SECURITY SYSTEMS SIMPLIFIED

Protecting Your
Home, Business,
and Car with
State-of-the-Art
Burglar Alarms

Steven Hampton

PALADIN PRESS
BOULDER, COLORADO

99

25530224

Also by Steven M. Hampton:
Secrets of Lock Picking
Advanced Lock Picking

Security Systems Simplified:
Protecting Your Home, Business, and Car with State-of-the-Art Burglar Alarms
by Steven Hampton

Copyright © 1992 by Steven M. Hampton

ISBN 0-87364-654-1
Printed in the United States of America

Published by Paladin Press, a division of
Paladin Enterprises, Inc., P.O. Box 1307,
Boulder, Colorado 80306, USA.
(303) 443-7250

Direct inquiries and/or orders to the above address.

PALADIN, PALADIN PRESS, and the "horse head" design
are trademarks belonging to Paladin Enterprises and
registered in the United States Patent and Trademark Office.

Contents

Introduction

here is a burglary in America every ten seconds. Dozens of lives and millions of dollars are lost each year to intruders who have little to lose. And the problem is not getting any better.

The best solution to this problem is to educate ourselves in the prevention of such an event. Most intruders certainly seem educated enough to know how to break into homes and businesses. It is time that homeowners and businesspeople have access to this information as well. In this way we may be able to reduce the amount of burglaries and intruder encounters in our neighborhoods and workplaces.

A basic understanding of intruder alarm systems can help you determine what type of system is right for your needs. Chances are that if you are reading this book, you have been a victim of such a crime. There is no way that can be fixed or forgotten. But there is a way to keep it from happening to you again.

The first step to security is information—knowing what system is best for you is half the battle. The rest will be up to the alarm installer. Beyond that, all you'll have to do is a quick monthly check of your system.

Currently, perimeter-type systems are popular. At some point, however, a countersystem will be developed and become common knowledge among thieves. As technologies evolve into the twenty-first century and become widely used, there will always be someone out there who figures out a way to safely defeat the system. As such, newer systems come into existence.

It's sad that the greatest threat to our personal privacy and security comes from fellow human beings. The "have-nots" take from the "haves" mostly because the have-nots feel they have a fundamental right to a sense of self-worth and value. If people feel that they cannot express their potency and value, there will be anger and distrust. When this is coupled with complications such as hunger and drug lust (the misdirected search for physical/spiritual unity), criminals will feel totally justified in their motives. Therefore, until society's problems have been dealt with effectively, security systems will be needed. Discouraging an intrusion in the first place may give a potential criminal another chance to think about his alternatives (at least that is what the author hopes for).

Although this information is technical, I have tried to put it in layperson's terms to make it understandable. Also, I have included an appendix of commonly used electronic symbols with their respective component drawings for identification. This will help you visualize an illustration of an electronic circuit without having to know or fully understand complex mathematics or established theories.

A schematic—a simple line drawing "blueprint" of a circuit—reveals all of the detailed information needed to build, test, or repair that circuit. On the other hand, a block diagram (sometimes referred to as a block schematic) represents a relationship or a sequence of events.

CHAPTER 1

History of Intruder Alarm Systems

F or centuries man has been trying to protect himself, his family, and his valuables from potential criminals. The ancient Egyptians invented the pin tumbler lock. It was constructed of wooden pegs (tumblers) in a block that could be slid across a door when the pegs were properly aligned. A large wooden key of sorts could be inserted into a hole. This raised the wooden pegs and, as the key was turned, scooted the wooden bar across the door to open it. The Egyptians also set up complicated mazes and deadly traps to protect the wealth they buried with their pharaohs in the pyramids and other tombs. Starting rumors about curses was also a way to cut out all the amateurs.

Because locks can be defeated and traps bypassed, man has found himself in need of a watch dog that never sleeps or takes bribes. With the advent in the late nineteenth century of electrical devices like the electromagnetic solenoid and relay coil, along with batteries (invented by Voltaire in the early eighteenth century, they were called piles back then and were composed of lead, copper, and zinc plates immersed or covered with acid), the basics for the modern intruder alarm became available.

The first true intruder alarm system was patented in 1889 by Edwin Holmes. It was installed for the American

District Telegraph Company in New York City. Literally thousands of systems were invented afterward, all on a few varying themes. Most of them were as simple as the breaking of an electrical circuit with a switch. This would release a relay that closed a set of contacts and sounded an alarm. The alarm was usually a bell or other loud noise-making device. The idea (still true for most small systems) was to scare, embarrass, or confuse the intruder.

As electrical circuits evolved into vacuum tube electronics with the advent of radio in the 1920s, burglar alarms gradually became more sophisticated as well. Vibration detectors, floor-mat pressure switches, and taut-wire devices were in common use among large businesses by the late 1930s.

In the mid-1940s, photoelectric systems, glass-break detectors, and proximity-type systems were used in high-security places. By 1949, when Dr. William Shockley and his team at Bell Labs developed the semiconducting transistor, burglar alarm systems available at the time suddenly became largely obsolete. Electronics became more efficient, durable, compact, and dependable.

The technological explosion of the 1960s yielded infrared and ultrasonic systems, along with microwave intrusion detectors in the 1970s and 1980s. Also in the 1970s, photoelectric systems took advantage of the infrared light emitting diode (LED) and the sophisticated high-speed switching logic of computers. In the 1980s, infrared pyroelectric elements were being used to sense an intruder's infrared radiation (body heat).

As new technology emerged, each system was considered state-of-the-art and virtually undefeatable by burglars. They were almost always very expensive, and only areas demanding high security could afford to use such innovative technology.

In the America of the 1960s, when ultrasonic systems were first introduced to the general public, few homes needed them; in that time of plenty (for most), homes were being burglarized only once every two minutes. As American society became more wholeheartedly materialistic and resources became more limited, even ultrasonic and infrared systems were not enough to stop the clever thief, as these systems had inherent weaknesses. But the most common problem with a large majority of them was that they were not installed or maintained properly. In fact, most alarm system failure today is due to these two factors. Deterioration of the system with age is an ally to the professional thief as long as he is aware of it. Most of them are.

As mentioned, the 1970s brought us LEDs and high-speed computer logic. In the 1980s, digital electronics allowed us to store even greater quantities of information. This led to the development of "smart" security systems that worked by comparing a set of norms against an actual event. This allowed computers to make decisions such as whether or not a coded-card user should be allowed entry or, when a television monitor picked up an intruder in the shadows of a protected area, whether or not to notify the guard on duty. Combined with even better infrared proximity detectors, this gave the burglar a lot to keep up with in the 1980s.

The 1990s should see an even bigger flood of new, high-tech intruder alarm systems. As crime increases at an alarming rate, more and more people will be concerned with personal safety. I suspect that the most effective and popular alarm systems will be simple, portable, and easy to use at home or on vacation.

CHAPTER 2

The Professional Burglar

t is estimated that well over 70 percent of all the burglaries committed in America are the result of the burglar "casing the joint." This is the act of observing the premises for an undetermined amount of time in order to assess the risk against the potential gains. If the place of business or residence looks secure, it is less likely to be a target. But what type of person is a burglar, and what distinguishes the professional from the amateur?

Basically there are three types, or classes, of burglar/intruder. The first is the amateur, accounting for about 75 percent of all burglars. These people generally are opportunists and hold down regular jobs. The second class of burglar is the semiprofessional. These people are somewhat successful at gaining entry without detection, and they make up approximately 23 percent of the total. The final class is the professional. They usually are skilled at lock picking, safe cracking, defeating electronic alarm systems, and so on. The professional burglar is seldom caught and is the subject of romantic stories of high adventure among thieves. But the professional burglar makes up only about 2 percent of the total. [1]

The amateur will try to get the job done quickly, usually within two to five minutes. The stolen article or articles are usually "fenced" or sold within an hour or two from the time they were taken. Professional burglars, on the other hand, take up to an hour or more to accomplish their deed. Their target often is of considerable value, which justifies the extra time and risk.

The average burglar prefers to avoid violence and will not resort to it unless he is startled or cornered. Therefore, most burglars like unoccupied locations: residences during the day and businesses at night. The professional burglar also realizes that the best time to steal is a few hours before sunrise. There are many reasons for this. The police usually are changing shifts about this time. If not, they are more likely to be tired. (It has been proven clinically that people are daytime beings and, even after many years of conditioning, still get groggy at three or four in the morning. Also, near the end of a shift one tends to feel a bit tired anyway.) For this reason, too, you may find police officers in need of a pick-me-up snack during this time. This is normal and not a reason to chide them about donut breaks (though some jokes I have heard about this subject are quite funny).

Beyond this, few employees arrive at a place of business before 5:00 A.M. Therefore, starting a job at 3:00 A.M. gives the burglar at least two hours before any employees drift in. But the most important reason that burglars prefer this time of day is that most everyone else is asleep. It is also quiet and dark—perfect conditions for a crime of this nature. This slight edge has helped to keep many burglars from getting caught. It should be noted, however, that in the wee hours of the morning the air is usually cooler and a little denser, so sound travels further. Air molecules are closer together when cooled, thus allowing the pressure of the sound waves to be passed on to other air molecules more efficiently. The sound doesn't actually travel faster; it just seems to be louder because more air molecules are being vibrated. Thus any noise made during a burglary in the early morning hours can be heard further away than during the day.

The best that can be expected from any intruder alarm system is to deter the amateur and occasional semiprofessional burglar. The professional burglar, on the other hand, usually has access to all kinds of technical (and nontechnical) information regarding alarm systems (which, by the way, is easier to get then most people suspect) and is also a multiskilled person. This person keeps abreast of the latest technological advances in alarm systems, locks, safes, computer hard- and software, and electronic components in general, not to mention security guard schedules and so forth. The professional "cat burglar" in particular has become a formidable predator of individual wealth. It is to the average homeowner's relief that professional burglars prefer small, valuable items like jewelry and not regular household goods.

Unfortunately, many people feel that the average criminal is lacking in intelligence. Yet many burglars are skilled in one or more technical fields, such as computerized bookkeeping, locksmithing, electronics, and fine mechanics. So intruder alarm systems should be working at all times when one is away since these skilled technicians will try their best to defeat them.

CHAPTER 3

Basic Security Measures

T echnology alone cannot stop the determined intruder, as electronic security systems are not capable of detecting an actual crime. They can only detect an activity that generally is associated with a crime. This is important to realize. The link between the two is purely technical, preventing intruder alarm systems from being 100-percent effective and allowing them to be defeated.

For example, an ultrasonic intrusion alarm system does not detect the actual presence of the intruder. It only detects motion in a protected area where no motion should be during that time of the day. But the intruder can defeat the alarm system by technical means before he commits the crime. If the above difference did not exist, the system could detect the intruder before he defeated it. Since this is not possible (as yet), concealment of the alarm system is to the home/business owner's advantage.

Intruder alarm systems must also be designed to fit the situation. Every home or office is different. Therefore there is no 100-percent effective system that one can purchase off-the-shelf for all security scenarios. Even the most sophisticated, expensive, mind-boggling, blinkity-light, whirlbeep system can be defeated. On the other hand, a $20 doorknob intruder alarm could be more reliable under certain circumstances.

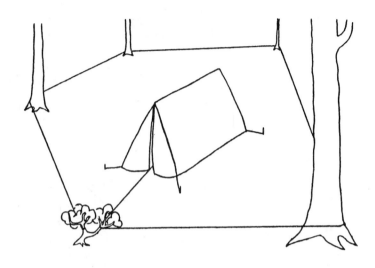

Figure 1. A simple campsite intruder alarm using a light test fishing line set six inches above the ground. A rubber band is then attached to the line and wrapped around the big toe of the camper.

Some alarm systems become nuisances and detect nonexisting crimes. For example, a $3,000 ultrasonic system can be tripped by a steam valve from a radiator, sounding a false alarm. Thus each system must be fine-tuned to respond only to human intruders, otherwise too many false alarms will force one to turn the system off permanently. False alarms are not only expensive but they bother the police, create unnecessary aging in the owner, and inspire one to drop-kick the whole damned system out the door.

Some experts estimate that more than 80 percent of alarm systems in use today are ineffective due to poor installation. Age, oxidation, dust, and mechanical wear are the other main causes of system failure—little or no maintenance and too many false alarms shut them down.

Most professional burglars know this, and home/business owners should know that they know this.

Another one of the main problems with most systems is the lack of knowledge upon installation. Even professional alarm installers are sometimes guilty of not being able to think like an intruder. In order to install a system properly, all angles must be observed carefully. A career burglar will spend hours, days, and even weeks contemplating your system. Most installers can't or won't do this, so you should. Hopefully this book will give you insight into criminal activity as well as the basic information you need to reduce your risk of becoming a victim.

Burglary is by far the most common type of crime today, and intrusion alarms account for more than 75 percent of all electronic security systems built (the others being personal alarms, infrared night-vision devices, etc.). When a system becomes popular or widely used, chances are very good that someone, somewhere has "cracked" it and has either sold or given the secrets away, thus disseminating the information. As time passes, more people become familiar with the system and the less effective it becomes.

Because of this, intruder alarm systems become progressively more complex. Measures follow countermeasures, and they "evolve" technically. This relentless process inspires new technology (and jobs). Nonetheless, the professional burglar will continue to develop methods to render current intrusion alarm systems ineffective. Therefore in the long run, there is no comfort in the fact that a system is difficult to defeat (though usage of your present system may be better than none at all).

For example, when the ultrasonic intrusion alarm was first introduced, it was considered by most to be virtually impossible to defeat. Yet it was well known that the Doppler effect responded not to the presence or motion of an object or being, but to the velocity of that object or being. It was also well known that in order to prevent false alarms from air currents or large insects, there had to be a lower limit to the velocity to which the ultrasonic system could respond. But few realized that the system responded primarily to reflections of the ultrasonic energy emitted and not simply from a directional source. Once this information became widespread, burglars began defeating ultrasonic systems by wearing soft, absorbent clothing and moving very slowly in the protected area.

(As ultrasonic systems evolved and became finely tuned for particular situations, burglars had to learn to move more slowly, to the point that it was no longer an effective way of defeating the system. The increased amount of time that it took to commit the crime wasn't worth the effort. Moving like a wet sloth in such a dangerous situation was too nerve-wracking, especially with adrenaline pumping through one's system.)

Even the most sophisticated intrusion alarm system made cannot protect the careless home/business owner. If one does not take the right precautions, the system is useless. When breaking and entering into a protected location, the burglar has a 20-percent chance that the alarm is not even activated. Either the owner did not turn it on or did not test it regularly, if at all, to be certain it was working properly.

That 20 percent in the intruder's favor gets him inside the premises, where he has plenty of time to accomplish a theft. His odds for success are even better considering that most systems are installed improperly, allow easy access to the main controls, or have no power-failure backup alarm. (Some systems use small batteries as backups in case of power failure, but these too need regular checking and/or testing.) Along with the fact that most door locks in use today are more than fifteen years old and can be picked easily with enough knowledge and experience (see my other books, *Secrets of Lock Picking* and *Advanced Lock Picking*, offered by Paladin Press), a professional intruder could be inside the premises undetected within twenty seconds.

The time it takes for the police to arrive on the scene when an alarm has been triggered also has great impact on the effectiveness of the system itself. Often, burglars will trip the alarm intentionally and hide at a safe distance to see how long it takes for the police to arrive. Since the police cannot travel at warp speed within city limits, there is a delay. But if the burglar does this four or fives times over a period of ten days to two weeks, he can safely assume (usually correctly) that the system will be turned off because of too many false alarms.

To cut down on false alarms, most cities bill the home/business owner $50 or more for every one turned in to the police. This can be the impetus for the home/business owner to shut his system down. If false alarms have become a problem for you, it is time to update your system—not only might it not be working properly, you may have a burglar casing your place. Have your system checked by a professional installer.

There are a few individuals out there who may feel challenged to defeat your new security system. They may not even consider whether or not their actions are legal, moral, or even dangerous. It's a battle of wits—you have set up barriers in their lives and they must outwit the system. From their perspective, it is like daring them to overcome this new obstacle even if it is none of their concern. The thrill of beating the system is of more value than any object they may steal. [2]

Despite these problems with electronic alarms, common sense is still the foundation of any security system. Quite often, the more complex the system becomes, the more likely simple mistakes can occur. Possible points of entry are overlooked, ignored, or considered improbable. But to the professional burglar, nothing is improbable. Of course there is a limit to what we can secure, and values have to be weighed so that you can employ a system that is effective yet affordable. Minimal maintenance is also highly desirable; the ideal system should be unaffected by dust or dirt, vibration, mechanical and electronic failure, or accidental bumping. (Infrared detectors, some proximity alarms, and microwave systems are relatively free of these problems—we will discuss them later.)

Easy access to the main control panel should be avoided (except, of course, with coded-entry systems). Install it in a closet or some other out-of-the-way place that house guests and servicemen don't normally frequent. If its location is evident, it is a simple matter for the potential burglar to either pick the lock to turn the unit off or to open and disable it. Some of the newer units have self-protection by means of vibration sensors or proximity detectors on the control box, while others just have an extra lock on the box so that two keys need to be turned simultaneously in order to access the system without sounding the alarm.

Many systems utilize an alarm cancel circuit; when someone enters the premises, they must enter a code into a small keyboard near the door to prevent the alarm from sounding. Usually, one has about thirty seconds to punch in the right code before the alarm goes off. This type of system is called a perimeter security terminal. At closing time another code is punched in to activate it, and one usually has another thirty seconds to leave and lock the door.

The main function of any security system is to make the crime difficult, time consuming, and attention getting. [3] Most burglars do not want to get caught, and they weigh the risk before committing the crime. Again, common sense is your best ally. Remember to lock doors and windows when you leave. Garage doors should also be checked. Some older garage door openers can be defeated simply by raising the door and forcing the chain and sprocket mechanism to slip. When buying a new garage door opener, make sure that its drive system is pinned together to prevent slippage. Basically, the drive mechanism should lock up when the unit is off. Most later models have this feature. This may sound simplistic, but I have noticed this potential security risk with many early garage door openers.

Careless habits such as not locking doors and windows are easily noticed. Leaving notes for delivery persons to leave merchandise inside unlocked doors is also not recommended. In the "old days" we could do this and there seldom was a problem, but times have changed.

Windows are particularly difficult to protect. Basement windows seem to be the preferred entry point of most residential burglars. These windows usually are casement style and open inward. Most intruders will try to open them by cutting a hole in the glass and unlocking the latch manually.

An effective way to hinder such attempts is to install barrel bolts at irregular intervals around the window frame. Three or more such latches are recommended for each window. The idea is to stall the intruder's efforts—he will cut a hole in the glass to reach and unlock the latch, only to find that there are other latches somewhere around the inside frame that he can't reach.

In high-crime areas, it is best to install shear or vibration sensors on basement windows and maintain them as part of a primary perimeter alarm system that includes the upper windows. Sadly, some homeowners must resort to placing bars on their basement windows.

You might want to consider installing sectional windows that open vertically, as shown in Figure 2. In most cases, this type of window is too narrow for someone to squeeze through. When the owner removes the handle cranks, it becomes extremely difficult to open from the outside.

Roof openings are another favorite point of entry for burglars, as they can enter with almost no chance of detection from the street. If you have skylights or dormer windows, protect them with piezoelectric sensors (vibration or shear detectors—we will discuss them in more detail

Figure 2. Burglar-resistant windows.

later). Put a high-security or pick-resistant padlock on any door or access port that needs a hasp. Only use a padlock that has a high-density steel body and a case-hardened shackle. Also, it should be either a pin tumbler lock with at least five pins or a rim cylinder lock with seven pins. Using a cheap padlock in such a vulnerable area is an open invitation that most burglars can't refuse. Consult your local locksmith for the best lock for your situation. (We will discuss locks in general in the next chapter.)

If you own a business, the back doors should be kept locked and barred. It is still somewhat controversial, but some people prefer to install double-locking cylinders on seldom-used doors. This means that the door is locked at all times from the inside as well as the outside; the key has to be used in order to both enter and exit the building. This may be good if you are trying to trap the intruder by limiting his escape routes, but you may be endangering the lives of your employees or family should a fire break out and the exit doors are locked.

In such cases, exit bars should be installed that can be

pushed opened from the inside during emergencies (see Fig. 3). Exit alarms can also be installed with a timer so that the alarm does not sound during normal business hours. The timer can be near the door in a locked control box; an intruder in a hurry to exit isn't going to spend time picking the control box lock and would rather trip the alarm and try to outrun apprehension. Again, check with your local locksmith about these security devices.

Figure 3. Exit alarm.

All alleys and rear entryways should be well lit. Caged light fixtures are a good investment. They come in a variety of styles and protect the light bulb from intentional breakage. A quarter-inch steel mesh is probably the surest bet against breakage from a low-caliber weapon. A mesh of smaller size may restrict the light.

Warning signs are also a good investment, but they should not lie. For example, don't put up a sign that reads "Security Guard On Premises" when you don't have one. If a burglar cases your place and doesn't see a guard on duty, he may assume that you are lying about any alarm systems that you may advertise as well (which is okay, but too many lies are obvious and have the reverse effect).

Television monitors are an excellent deterrent in some low-traffic, rear-entry areas such as back alleys. But one of the main problems with using fake TV cameras is that semiprofessional burglars have learned that throwing a pebble at the monitor's casing can determine whether it is operating or a fake. A real monitor will have a solid sound to it; a fake will sound hollow, like an empty coffee can.

Keeping debris and trash cleared from the back entry helps by eliminating hiding places for potential intruders. Boxes should be broken down if possible. Stack barrels no more than two high and close against the wall to reduce their use as barricades or hiding places. This forces an intruder to take the top barrels down if he decides to hide in one, which would cause a lot of noise.

Make sure that your windows are locked before closing up. Believe it or not, many get left open. Assign the task to a dependable employee and make it clear that it should become a concrete routine—as if his or her job depended on it. Tell him that you have the utmost faith in his dependability. This will make most employees try hard to not let you down and remember to do it.

Also, if you have a perimeter alarm system for the windows, make certain that the sensors are in working condition. You can also assign someone to check or test them once a month or during inventory time.

Warning stickers on windows also help to deter break-ins. In most cases sensors can be seen on the window glass, but amateurs may not know what they are.

It should be noted here that it is illegal to design or use an intruder-deterrent device that harms or kills the intruder. Property owners who do this could find themselves facing charges of second-degree murder, as occurred in a case in Denver, Colorado, in early 1990. Another case occurred in Florida in 1987—the owner went to prison. Deadly force cannot be used to protect one's property in most, if not all, states. Deadly force in this case refers to shotguns rigged up behind doors, for instance.

If your business deals directly with cash, leave the safe, cash box, or money drawer open and empty when closing up in the evening. Also, leave a "night light" (40 to 60 watts) on over the cash box or safe area to eliminate any doubts about whether or not there is cash on the premises. A 60-watt light source should be bright enough to allow someone to see inside the window from across the street.

It should be made clear to employees that any article taken from the premises must be logged in or verbally accounted for with an immediate supervisor. This will help to keep down company losses caused by internal theft.

Employers should also remember that although losses will be great if one doesn't utilize proper security measures, employees may feel uncomfortable and productivity may drop if security is too tight. A happy medium must be found based on common sense. Some people take it as an insult to their integrity if you suddenly hire security guards and set up elaborate alarm systems without first meeting with them and explaining the situation. In the same way, if you are in the retail business, you don't want to scare your customers off. Also, beefing up your security measures may force you to raise your prices to maintain an accustomed cash flow, and this will also drive your customers away to other stores. So one should look at as many angles as possible when deciding to improve security in the workplace.

The home/business owner needs to develop the attitude that it can happen to him or her. The odds are that someone will try to break into your home or office within the next five years. The best you can do is to protect yourself with an intrusion alarm system tailored to your needs.

CHAPTER 4

Locking Mechanisms

ince most professional burglars can pick locks quickly and quietly, and even high-security locks can be drilled or otherwise defeated, it is imperative to have a dependable intruder alarm system when security is essential. Yet simple things can be done to improve security at home and in the office. For example, if you have a knob lock on your door, be certain that it has a "dead-bolt" type latch. This is a small bar that lies alongside the latching bolt and helps to prevent the lock from being opened by use of a plastic card or other thin item (see Fig. 4). Notice I said, "helps to prevent." With correct manipulation, even this won't stop a determined intruder, but it will stop nearly all of the amateurs.

There are a few common misconceptions regarding dead-bolt locks. The first and most important myth is that they cannot be picked. This is untrue, since they use the same locking cylinders as regular knob locks. It is the latching mechanisms that are different. The main advantage of a dead bolt-type lock is that its latch is not spring-loaded and it cannot be pushed back with a card like those of knob locks. The cylinder has to turn before the latch can be pulled back.

Also, prying on the door jamb will not spring the door open if it has a locked dead bolt on it. The bolts usually

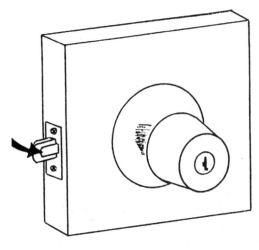

Figure 4. A dead-bolt-type latching door.

are one-inch long, and with such a long throw, popping open the door is not likely. If mounted properly, these locks make your door stronger and tougher to kick in.

If the house is two or more stories tall and is more than fifteen years old, chances are that the foundation has settled and the door jamb (or frame) has spread apart slightly. On most knob locks, this separates the latch from the strike plate in the jamb and allows one to push a locked door open easily just by leaning on it. Check your doors for this potential problem; burglars do. If you have a spreading door jamb, install or have installed a dead-bolt lock with at least one-inch travel and remember to use it. You may also want to call your locksmith to see about repairing the door jamb itself. Since some semiprofessional burglars commonly use the technique of "jamb spreading" with an auto jack or similar device, it is highly recommended that such problems be fixed.

In areas of high pedestrian traffic, the amateur will sometimes "tape-a-latch." Placing electrical or duct tape over the latch of an exit door allows the door to be opened from the outside later in the day or that evening. This trick was nationally publicized in 1972 during the Watergate scandal. A security guard removed some tape shortly after an unknown intruder placed it over the latch of an exit door. But the intruder did a foolish thing—he returned and retaped the latch. He was apprehended because he stuck to his original plan and entered the compromised door later that day. "What is also embarrassing was this government official's total lack of professionalism,"

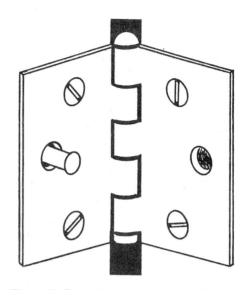

Figure 5. Securing exposed door hinges.

remarked a friend of mine. "He could have at least picked the lock."

Door hinges also can be a vulnerable point. Many times a door between a shed or a garage and a house will have the hinge pins on the outside of the door. Burglars can remove the door simply by tapping out the hinge pins. Note in Figure 5 that one of the screws has been removed and replaced with a large finishing nail. The corresponding hole on the other side of the hinge has been drilled to allow the head of the nail to fit into it when the door is closed. When this is done to the top and bottom hinges, the hinge pins can still be removed but the door will remain secure.[4]

Installing pick-resistant locks is one of the best things a home/business owner can do to ensure security. If you just bought a home, you should change all of the outside locks anyway; you never know who has a key to your house. You don't have to go out and buy expensive locks—pin tumbler locks (the most common type of front

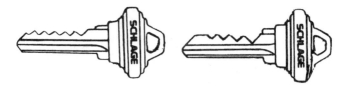

Figure 6. The lock to the key on the left is easy to pick. The lock to the key on the right is very difficult to pick.

door lock) can be rekeyed by your local locksmith to make picking them more difficult than they normally would be. Mushroom and spool pins, for instance, can be used in the lock, which make picking the lock a real hassle. Also, keying the last few tumblers higher than the front three will tend to cause a lock-picking tool to jam in the lock's cylinder (see my *Secrets of Lock Picking* for more information). This slows the intruder down greatly; usually he will give up after three to five minutes and go on to easier pickings.

If you want to discover whether or not your lock has been picked while you were out, look for a fine dusting of brass filings near the bottom of the keyway, in the front of the lock, and on the floor directly below it. Sometimes you'll see bright scratch marks on the bottom of the front pin (or wafer) tumbler. Since nearly all lock picks are harder than the brass of the pins, telltale marks will remain until the key has been used a few times. But remember, this may not necessarily mean that the break-in attempt was successful.

CHAPTER 5

Types of Intrusion Alarm Systems

here are three basic types of intrusion alarm systems. The first is called a proprietary alarm system. It functions with an on-site, central station that monitors various detectors or systems throughout the premises. A proprietary alarm system employs security guards who are dispatched to the scene of a suspected intrusion.

The second type of intrusion alarm system is called a central station alarm system. It is similar to a proprietary system except that all of the alarm circuits are tied to an off-site central station by radio or telephone lines, where they are monitored by security personnel.

The third type of intrusion alarm system is called a local system, which is simply an on-site system that is self-contained.

Let's take a look at each type of system. Proprietary alarms systems are used widely in universities and large manufacturing plants that employ their own security forces. Some military and most government facilities also use this type of system. A proprietary system can use many different types of detectors within its domain. For example, a security guard can monitor television cameras, an infrared sensor array, an isolated ultrasonic detector or two, as well as a proximity system protecting a line of filing cabinets. Each system is designed and set up to best protect a particular area. Usually one guard can monitor the entire system and can thus dispatch other guards to investigate a violation of the premises.

Some proprietary systems are set up so that when a guard patrols a facility, a special meter he carries records the time that he checks in at each patrol station along the route. If the guard encounters trouble and takes more time than is necessary to make his rounds, an alarm will sound and other guards will be dispatched to assist the first. This subsystem of the proprietary system, called a supervisory alarm system, also allows the plant manager to obtain a printed record of each time a particular gate or door is opened or closed. In this way, any unauthorized entry can be pinpointed. These systems are mostly computer controlled now.

The central station alarm system is similar to the proprietary system except that its nerve center is an off-site security company. Again, each protected area has its own intrusion detector, and all are consolidated into a multiple input circuit and monitored via telephone lines or, in special high-security cases, radio link. This type of system is less expensive to maintain and is usually used where security problems are moderate. Fire alarm circuits are often tied into these systems as well.

It should be noted that many central station alarm systems have audio monitors. When an alarm is received, a guard at "headquarters" can actually listen in and record to verify an intrusion.

The third type of intrusion alarm system, the local alarm system, basically consists of isolated units that use a bell or siren to sound an alarm when an intruder has tripped the system. One general disadvantage of a local alarm system is that the burglar/intruder knows when his presence has been detected, giving him enough time to escape. In many cases, the police arrive after the intruder has fled the scene, usually with something of value.

The main advantage of a local alarm system is that it

is cost-effective; it offers the best protection available for the price. It is even more effective if neighbors agree to keep an open ear for any tripped alarm when the owner is not at home. Check with neighborhood-watch programs being implemented in various communities. If your area doesn't have one, start one.

Another factor associated with alarm bells and especially sirens is their ability to provoke a powerful psychological reaction. For example, when an alarm is tripped, an ear-splitting siren will upset most intruders. The siren also makes it difficult for the intruder to hear the approach of police vehicles. This alone is sometimes enough to force him to leave before completing his task. When combined with flashing and blinding lights, it can produce physiological effects that are of great advantage to the home/business owner.

The complexity and effectiveness of an intrusion alarm system is directly proportional to the value of what is being protected; the larger the risk, the better the system. Since it is to the home/business owner's advantage to detect an intruder's presence as soon as possible, proper installation is essential. Since this is such a broad subject, being that each situation is unique, I can only lay down general guidelines as to what is considered by most professional installers to be a proper installation.

The details of your particular system should not be divulged to anyone other than your installer (for extra security, some refuse to keep a copy of a customer's system on file). Most intrusion alarm experts treat their installations much like that of a locksmith who comes in to reset the combination lock on a safe. The locksmith will write the new combination on the palm of his hand, allow the owner to copy it, and then immediately wash his hands with a mild solvent. No other copy of the combination is made—that is left up to the safe owner's discretion.

In the same way, the availability of alarm system plans is left to the owner's discretion. But because such systems can be so complex, the installer usually keeps a (or the only) copy in his locked files. In order for a thief to get his hands on your alarm plans, he would have to know many things: who installed the system, when, and where they keep the plans and schematics.

As mentioned above, the best time to detect an intruder is as soon as possible, i.e., when he is at the edge of your premises. This is where a perimeter protection system is advisable. This system consists of detectors on doors, windows, gates, and fences. The idea is to initiate an alarm before the perpetrator has a chance to enter the building, where he can operate in seclusion. Businesses and stores that are closed at night require this type of protection. Just remember that if you make your gates and fences too sensitive to human contact, you could end up with a lot of false alarms caused by innocent passersby.

But even these types of systems can't offer 100-percent protection. There are many cases in which burglars have entered a building through the walls, floors, or ceilings. Also, perimeter-type detection systems are useless against the "stay-behind" burglar who enters a place of business during regular business hours, locates a hiding place, and remains there until it is closed and locked up. Then when it is safe, he comes out, takes what he has come for, and leaves, tripping the perimeter alarm on the way out. Of course when the police arrive, the burglar is long gone.

The next line of defense for the home/business owner is the isolated area protection system. The isolated area system detects the presence of an intruder either by ultrasonic, infrared, or microwave emissions and acts as a major backup for the perimeter protection system. These systems will pick up any stay-behinds who decide that it is safe to move around. With isolated area protection, you can also protect areas in certain parts of a factory and leave the remaining sections of the plant open for night operation.

A third type of local alarm system is called spot protection. This is a detector that triggers an alarm when someone or something touches or comes near a protected object. Filing cabinets, safes, and display cases containing jewelry are often protected in this way. This type of system is usually backed up with an isolated area and/or a perimeter protection system.

Spot protection devices include proximity detectors, floor-mat switch arrays, mercury switches (tilt or motion detectors), and weight-sensing devices (a type of floor-mat switch array; these are pads used to protect small objects such as rare museum pieces in display cases), as well as limited infrared systems such as door announcers (which sound a bell when someone breaks a light beam upon entering a room). In some stores, a manager may install a multicircuit switchboard in or near his desk. A switch can be used to disarm the siren and activate a red light or buzzer in his office instead. This way he can monitor the accessing of the cabinet or cash drawer during regular business hours. Just before closing up, he can switch back to the siren circuit.

CHAPTER 6

Detectors – General Information

A n ideal intrusion detector would respond only to the presence of a human and not to animals or large insects. It would not respond to changes in temperature and humidity, or to the occasional breeze, rain, or unrelated vibration. Unfortunately, most intrusion alarm systems are too sensitive and respond to such irrelevant influences. When a system is designed and employed, it should not respond to any thing or event other than the presence of a human intruder. And it has to respond every time. This is a lot to ask of a technical system—to distinguish between a man and a mouse, or a breeze—and then always be prepared to announce that to the world. As simple as that may sound, it is actually a very complex task for a machine to do. And again, attention to the initial installation is required if that task is to be done properly.

This complex task that intrusion alarm systems must perform is done with electronics, and I have attempted to clarify schematic diagrams and other data as much as possible with the appendix at the back of this book. Each circuit presented in schematic form includes a brief description of its operation. This should help the layperson to at least have an idea of what the schematics are about. There is enough information provided with each circuit for an electronic technician to build that particular circuit. But again, proper installation is an important factor in the use of any device, and the author and publisher cannot take responsibility for any circuit you may build from this book.

The human body blocks out relatively strong light, so a photoelectric system can be arranged to detect the presence of an intruder. Humans and animals also emit infrared energy in the form of body heat caused by metabolism. This can be detected with infrared sensors.

In most cases, objects cannot be stolen without making some kind of noise, so audio detection systems have been designed to pick up sounds above normal background noise. These are computer-monitored.

Another characteristic of a human intruder is that he will disturb ultrasonic or electromagnetic fields in his passage. Thus ultrasonic and microwave intrusion detectors as well as capacitive proximity detectors work on this principle.

Finally, there are four basic parts or stages to most

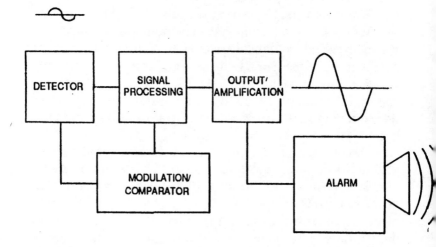

Figure 7. Block diagram of the four basic parts of an alarm system. The modulator/comparator can be used to establish signal reference for the detector input.

intrusion alarm systems. The first is the detector, which picks up either a change in motion, vibration, sound, body heat, or capacitance. The second stage is called the signal processing circuit. Here the incoming signal from the detector is either clarified or verified, whichever applies (sometimes both). The third stage is the latching circuit (though some systems use an amplifier circuit). This acts like a switch that, in most cases, turns on when a signal is input from the signal processor (some systems have this latching circuit turned off in order to prevent an intruder from merely cutting wires to disable the system).

Mechanical and solid-state relays commonly are used at this stage. Solid-state relays are units that contain semiconductors engineered to act like high-speed switches in most cases. Since these "switches" have no mechanical contacts, they have a dependable and long life. The switching occurs on a molecular level where a small electrical current can control a much larger electrical current. Technically, this is not amplification since all the circuit can do in a solid-state relay is either turn absolutely on or absolutely off. But the process is virtually the same as amplification.

The last of the four basic parts of an intrusion alarm system is the alarm itself. This can be either a siren, bell, horn, telephone dialer, or radio link to a security center.

Some specialized systems use a fifth circuit—either a modulator, which forms the signal so that the intruder cannot duplicate it, or a comparator, which sets references for the detector. Comparators are used in computer circuits; you can find a good example of such a system with a perimeter-type security terminal (see Fig. 19).

CHAPTER 7

Electromechanical Detectors

E lectromechanical detectors were the first types of intrusion alarm systems ever used. They have since evolved and are still used today because of their simplicity, dependability, and low cost.

DOOR AND WINDOW SWITCHES

Surprisingly, one of the simplest yet most effective electromechanical detector switches is the plunger-type door switch. If mounted properly, it is very difficult to defeat because the door has to be open in order to get to it. Of course once the door is opened, the door switch triggers the alarm.

This switch should be mounted in the door jamb on the hinge side of the door. Should an intruder locate the exact position of the switch, however, he may succeed in defeating it by slipping in a thin piece of steel plate to depress and hold down the plunger. The plate is bent at a right angle and has two or three holes in one side, through which he taps in a few nails or runs a few screws. This holds the plunger switch in the off position while he picks the lock on the door and enters undetected.

If the door has an overlapping edge or seals tight when closed, the alarm cannot be foiled in this way. If your door does have a gap on the hinged side, you may want to mount the microswitch with a right-angled

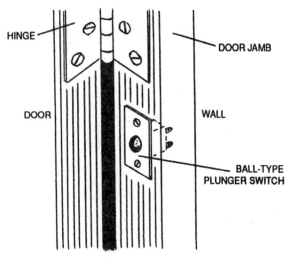

Figure 8. Door switch.

bracket above the door instead—this way the switch gets tripped every time the door is opened.[5]

Magnetic reed switches are a more reliable way of protecting doors and windows. The principle is simple: when two parallel ferrous (iron) materials are brought into a magnetic field, they attract each other, making contact (see Fig. 9). In most commercial reed switches, the contacts are mercury wetted and sealed within a small glass cylinder with a vacuum for long life. They are virtually silent as well.

The permanent magnet is mounted on the movable surface of the door or window. The reed switch and its two wire leads are mounted on the door jamb or window frame. When the door or window is opened, the magnetic field is removed from the reed switch, opening the contacts. This in turn can activate a relay that closes its contacts and sounds the alarm.

WINDOW FOIL
Metallic window foil systems are among the most

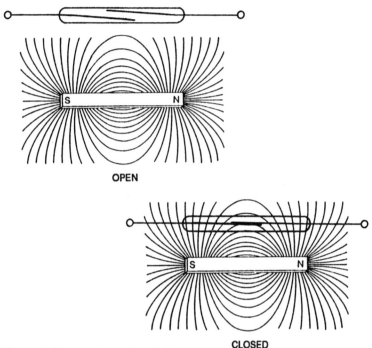

Figure 9. Magnetic reed switch.

widely used perimeter detectors. The foil has an adhesive backing and is part of an electrical circuit. If the window (or glass door) is cracked or broken, the foil is sheared and the circuit opens. This in turn switches on the input or the base of a transistor, which activates a relay down the circuit, sounding the alarm.

Some burglars have defeated these types of perimeter systems by drilling a pair of small holes with a diamond-tipped drill bit at the juncture of the pickup leads (current systems now use a special terminal block to help prevent this). The holes penetrate the foil without breaking it, and a spring-loaded treble hook is forced into each. These are then shorted together and the window is broken without tripping the alarm.

But since all conductors have a certain amount of

resistance-to-current flow, we can measure this resistance for different materials, shapes, lengths, etc. So some window foil protection circuits employ the foil as a resistor: if any section is shorted along the circuit path, the reduced resistance of the path on the transistor's base side will reverse its bias and turn the transistor on, sounding the alarm. In other words, the foil acts like a resistor, keeping the circuit input transistor in forward bias. (We will discuss these types of circuits in more detail later on.)

A clever burglar can estimate the resistance of a window circuit (the resistance of aluminum foil tape is approximately 17 ohms-cmil/ft., or 17 ohms of electrical resistance per circular millimeter of every foot of wire) and set a potentiometer (or "pot" as it is commonly called) to the estimated resistance with a volt/ohmmeter. He can also buy some window foil, measure its resistance with an ohmmeter, and set the pot accordingly. He then

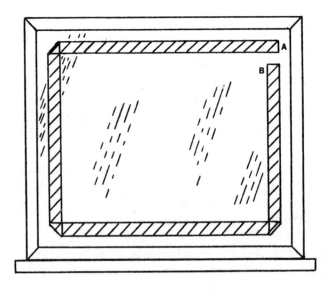

Figure 10. Typical window foil installation.

jumpers the pot to the terminal block while breaking the window. Luckily, not many burglars will go to this much trouble since the process is time-consuming and requires a large percentage of guesswork on the actual footage of the foil tape. Also, different brands of foil have different resistive values per foot. Finally, breaking the window while simultaneously making an electrical contact requires a lot of practiced skill.

Sometimes a burglar will break in by taping up the window glass with duct tape, covering it with a heavy coat or blanket to muffle the sound, then breaking it with a shoulder or knee. But the most popular technique is by cutting a circular hole with a glass cutter (at least six inches in diameter) and tapping it out, enabling the intruder to reach in and open the window latch. (By the way, the hole has to be round. A square or triangular hole will break the entire pane—and the image of someone cutting a square hole in glass is hilarious to me anyway since glass tends to break perpendicular to applied forces.) Even so, the technique required to quietly cut a hole in glass is not an easy one to master. High-strength plate glass is now widely used in doors and some windows, and cutting holes in it is nearly impossible.

Figure 10 is an example of a simple window foil arrangement. The conductive foil has adhesive backing. A terminal block, also with adhesive backing, is fastened to points A and B. Should the window break, the foil opens and the alarm sounds. But this arrangement has a serious drawback: intruders can see the foil junction points A and B. Therefore the foil should be arranged in such a way that the intruder cannot determine where the junction is, as is illustrated in Figure 11. The three "fake junctions" should be located out of view of any potential burglar, usually along the inside of the window frame. This will make the job of defeating the system four times more difficult.

One of the most common maintenance problems with

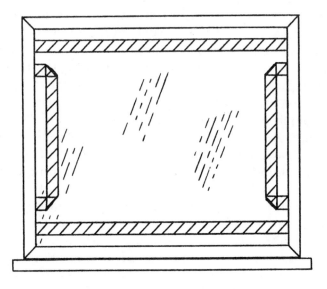

Figure 11. The proper way to install window foil.

window foil is that it is subject to wear through abrasion from window washing. Also be aware that if the connections to the foil are soldered directly to the wires, there will be a good chance that the connections will not last long. This could cause false alarms (which always happen late at night it seems). As was mentioned, terminal blocks designed for this purpose will prevent this from happening. Still, window foil systems need regular inspections and occasional repair.

In most cases, a window foil system is effective in keeping out nearly all amateur burglars. Yet in high-crime areas, these systems should always be backed up with another local alarm system such as a motion detector (infrared, ultrasonic, or, if resources permit, microwave) or a presence detector like a proximity system. (We will discuss these systems later as well.)

GLASS-BREAK AND VIBRATION SENSORS

Glass-break and vibration sensors are sometimes used to detect when someone is trying to manipulate or breach the surface of a window or glass door. In such circumstances they are very effective and very difficult to defeat.

Glass-break sensors work by the piezoelectric principle—when a quartz crystal is squeezed or otherwise mechanically distorted, it produces a brief, minute burst of electricity. This can be picked up and amplified to set off an alarm. These are called solid-state glass-break sensors, or sometimes shear sensors.

When using such detectors, it is wise to keep tree branches and other foliage clear of the windows so the wind does not cause false alarms. In rare cases, loud noises have also been known to set them off. Be sure that your sliding glass doors and windows are not subject to such circumstances by keeping tree limbs and such pruned.

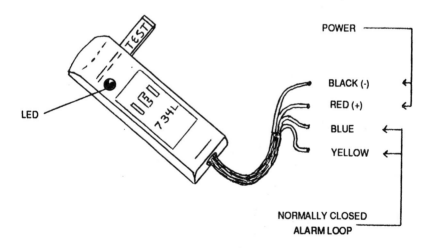

Figure 12. This glass-break detector is externally powered with an isolated alarm circuit and indicating LED. The alarm is normally held energized so loss of power gives fail-safe alarm. No external processor or interface is required.

PRESSURE-SENSITIVE FLOOR MATS

Another popular type of electromechanical switching system is the pressure-sensitive floor mat. Most units work by the closing of one or more "bubble switches" (like the kind used on computer keyboards) set up in a matrix inside a heavy-duty rubber mat. Whenever someone steps on the mat, one or more of these switches close. These mats are often used in small stores and repair shops to let someone working in the back know that a customer is in the front of the store. More frequently, they are used as local intruder alarm systems placed in front of vulnerable objects like filing cabinets, safes, or jewelry cases. This type of spot protection is an inexpensive way to complement a perimeter-type system such as window foil intrusion alarms.

TILT AND VIBRATION SWITCHES

Electromechanical detectors have a wide variety of uses limited only by one's imagination. The vibration sensor in Figure 13a uses a coil of fine, insulated copper wire wrapped around a nonmagnetic slug.[6] This is suspended by a spring into a magnetic field supplied by the permanent magnets. When the coil is moved by the inertia of the mass in motion, a small electrical current is generated and sent off to be amplified, which then sounds the alarm. This particular device is called an electromechanical tilt sensor and is very sensitive. A newer version of the device is illustrated in Figure 13b and uses electrolytic chemicals to sense gravity. These tilt sensors are extremely sensitive and can operate on separate axes.

A simple mechanical vibration switch is illustrated in Figure 13c. When the switch is at rest, it is electrically open (off). If it is even slightly bumped or vibrated, the mass moves, bumping into the contact on the bottom of the device. This type of sensor has been around for some time and was used in pinball machines as a tilt sensor before mercury switches were incorporated. They are

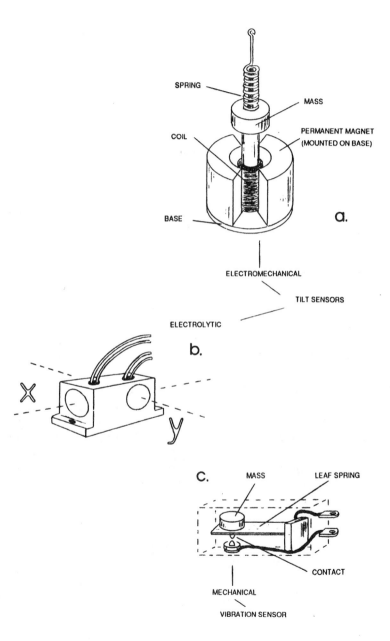

SPRING

MASS

COIL

PERMANENT MAGNET
(MOUNTED ON BASE)

BASE

a.

ELECTROMECHANICAL

TILT SENSORS

ELECTROLYTIC

b.

X

y

c.

MASS

LEAF SPRING

CONTACT

MECHANICAL

VIBRATION SENSOR

Figure 13. Tilt and vibration sensors.

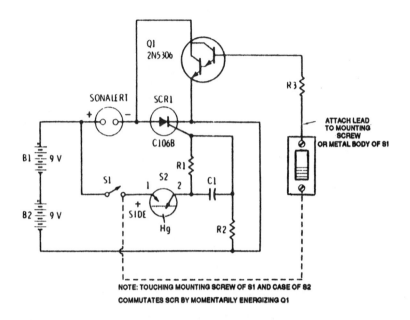

NOTE: TOUCHING MOUNTING SCREW OF S1 AND CASE OF S2
COMMUTATES SCR BY MOMENTARILY ENERGIZING Q1

Figure 14. Hotel room alarm. Alarm mounted is in a flashlight-shaped cylinder and positioned on floor of hotel room in such a way that it would be knocked over by an intruder opening the door. Mercury switch S2 then triggers the SCR and activates Mallory SC-628P pulsed Sonalert alarm. Circuit latches on and can be turned off only by use of Darlington-amplifier touch switch. Connection from the base of Darlington to positive terminal must be made through fingertips (as shown by dashed line) in order to silence alarm. Once silenced, S1 can be opened to disconnect latch so alarm can be moved. Other applications include protection of unattended luggage. C1 is 0.1µF, R1 is 1 megohm, R2 is 1K, R3 is 39K, and S2 is mercury element removed from GE mercury toggle switch. (From *The Build-It Book of Safety Electronics*, by R.F. Graf and G.J. Whalen, published by Howard W. Sams, Indianapolis, IN, 1976, p. 19-24.)

now commonly used in protecting automobiles—if the car is started or jacked up so that a tire can be stolen, the switch will set off the alarm.

Mercury switches (similar to the ones used in furnace

thermostats) are often used inside safes and cabinets. During normal use the switch remains open. It activates if someone tries to steal the safe or cabinet—the small pool of mercury rolls away from its resting place inside the switch and makes contact with two terminals, completing the circuit and sounding the alarm. Small, portable versions of the mercury switch alarm system are available and can simply be hung on the inside door knob; if the door is opened without turning the unit off, an ear-piercing alarm is sounded. [7] These types of travel alarms are becoming popular with vacationers.

TAUT-WIRE INTRUSION ALARMS

Another simple yet effective means of perimeter protection is the taut-wire intrusion alarm system. (An even simpler yet convenient form of this system used by campers in bear country is illustrated in Figure 1.)[8] This system uses a wire strung taut around the perimeter. The wire is black and thin, such as a painted piano wire, which makes it difficult to detect. It is usually mechanically connected to a snap-action microswitch (see Appendix) via a spring. When tension increases or decreases, the switch is thrown and triggers the alarm.

Thermal expansion and contraction of the wire could cause many false alarms, so commercial units use temperature-compensating mechanisms that add tension when the weather gets hot and relax the wire when the weather cools. Sudden changes to the wire tension are

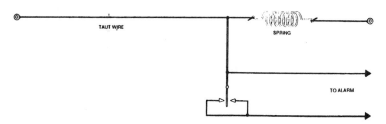

Figure 15. Taut-wire intrusion alarm.

not tolerated by the system and will cause the alarm to sound. There have been cases where a sudden cold snap (25 degree or more drop) has set these systems off.

ADVANTAGES

An important advantage of electromechanical detectors is that they are simple and highly dependable. If properly installed and periodically checked, they can be an effective yet inexpensive way to protect your premises. An electromechanical system is a good front line of defense (and in some cases a backup) for local alarm systems and spot protection devices. Since they are more visible than other types of systems, amateurs and semiprofessional burglars will notice them and stay away. On the other hand, a professional thief may defeat the electromechanical perimeter system and, feeling safe, walk right into a spot-protection system, setting off the alarm. So another advantage to an electromechanical system is that it can set up the intruder for detection and arrest.

Simple electromechanical systems also have the advantage of versatility. Switches can be located throughout the store, for example, and be tripped by employees should a robbery occur during store hours. Cash registers can be set up with pressure-sensitive switches that will trigger a silent alarm in the manager's office should an abnormally large sum of cash be removed.

DISADVANTAGES

Electromechanical intrusion detectors have limitations. They cannot cover the entire premises. One could protect all of the windows and doors with switches, tape, etc., but a clever thief could still get in via the walls, floor, or ceiling. So electromechanical intrusion alarm systems are seldom used when maximum security is required. If they are used for maximum security, they are always backed up with other systems.

Many times these systems are not only poorly installed, but are done so with little imagination. The sensors are visible when they should not be and invisible when they should not be, as some sensors need to be seen by the amateur burglar to act as a deterrent while others need to be well hidden in case the intruder defeats the perimeter system.

When using microswitches, wear and tear on door switches must be monitored. Most main exit doors are opened and closed several times a day. After about ten years, that's more than 25,000 cycles, and this will wear out the best of switches (except for magnetic reed switches, of course).

But in reality, most electromechanical systems are dependable and cost-effective. They offer good protection against the amateur and semiprofessional burglar and have been known to catch a few professionals too. Don't overlook these versatile devices when designing your own system with a competent installer.

CHAPTER 8

Basic Latching
Circuits

O ne of the oldest intrusion detectors still
in use today is the electromechanical
switch used on doors and windows (foil
tape is considered a switch of sorts).
Whenever something happens with the
mechanical side of the system, the
electrical side either goes on or off
(changes electrical status). This status
change is amplified down the circuit and sets off the
alarm. Yet it would be a simple matter for the burglar to
violate the switch, set off the alarm momentarily, and
reconnect it when inside to silence the alarm. Latching
circuits were developed to prevent intruders from
defeating an alarm system in this way.

The simple perimeter system in Figure 10, for example,
has some disadvantages. The alarm can be silenced by
shorting out points A and B. All an intruder has to do is cut
a hole in the glass and reach in to jumper points A and B,
break the window, and enter. What is even more important
to note is that the thief can also simply break the window,
then short out the terminal block to silence the alarm. That
is why the use of the latching-type switch evolved into
widespread instrusion alarm use. Once it is activated,
shorting the terminal block will not silence the alarm.

Mechanical-type relays were the first devices used
to guarantee that, once activated, the system could not

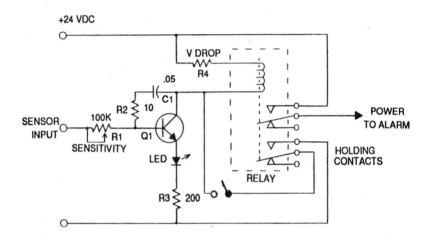

Figure 16. Latching relay circuit. Once relay has been activated by Q1, a ground is maintained (latched) through the relay's holding contacts.

be shut down by the intruder. A relay is basically an electromagnet that pulls a hinged flap (armature) down, moving sets of electrical contacts with it. These contacts can either separate (opening the circuit) or join (closing the circuit).

A simple way to use a relay as an electronic latch is illustrated in Figure 16. When the transistor is switched on by an input signal, current can flow from the power supply (VDC) through the relay to ground, completing the circuit path. If the input signal is stopped, the alarm remains on because the relay is now getting its ground from the relay-hold contacts. The alarm will sound until S1 is opened momentarily, removing the ground from the relay and resetting it.

The latching switch circuit shown in Figure 17 is another good, basic example that uses a silicon-controlled rectifier (SCR) as part of the electronic latch.[9]

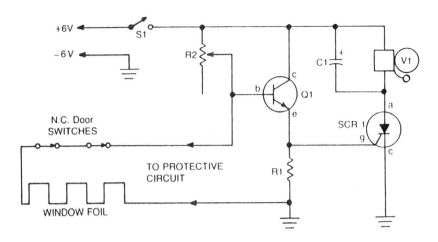

Figure 17. Latching switch circuit. When the protective circuit is interrupted (opened), the alarm sounds. To set the circuit, adjust R2 (with protective circuit open) for 1 V across R1.

Here's how it works: with a 6-volt power source, the circuit remains inactive until an opening of the "protective circuit" occurs. Transistor Q1 then turns on (just like the transistor in the circuit in Figure 16), which then sends a signal to the gate (g) of SCR 1. This in turn allows current to flow through the anode and cathode elements of the SCR via the alarm bell, sounding the bell itself. Reestablishing the protective circuit of the foil or door switch (by closing the door, for instance) will not silence the alarm because once SCR 1 has fired, it continues to conduct until the 6-volt power source has been disconnected (S1). This resets the alarm. R2 is a setup function potentiometer and is used to adjust the circuit in accordance with the resistive length of the protective circuit. It sets the bias for Q1. R1 sets reference for the SCR, and C1 suppresses arcing of the bell's contacts for longer life.

A more sophisticated version of the above alarm circuit is illustrated in Figure 18. [10] Essentially, this circuit is the same except that it employs an integrated circuit (IC)

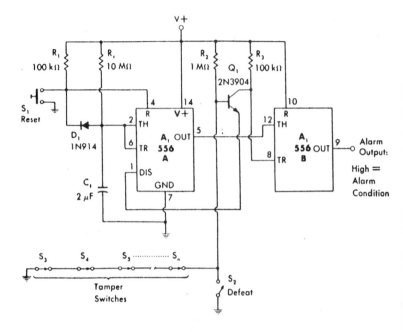

Figure 18. A more sophisticated latching circuit, a window-foil alarm. The combination of power-up mono MVBR and latch, using both sections of 556 timer, drives output line high when sensor circuit is opened at door or window switch or by breaking foil on glass. Once alarm is triggered, reclosing of sensor has no effect; S must be closed momentarily after restoring sensor circuit to turn alarm off. Circuit includes 22-S power-up delay that prevents triggering of alarm when it is first turned on. (From *Timer Cookbook*, by Howard W. Sams, published by Howard W. Sams, Indianapolis, IN, 1977, p. 231-232.)

or "chip." One-half of the chip (section A) is used as a latching switch while the other half (section B) drives the alarm. This circuit also uses a 22-second power-up delay to prevent triggering of the alarm when the system is turned on. S1 must be closed momentarily to reset the system. S2 is a defeat switch and should be well-hidden and not labeled. The voltage required by this circuit can be 9 to 15 volts DC. Alarm output can be used to drive a relay, which then triggers the alarm.

CHAPTER 9

Perimeter Security Terminals

The detector of a perimeter intrusion alarm can be likened to sense perception and the latching circuit to the heart. But in order for a system to be complete and totally effective, it needs a brain. And that's how modern perimeter intrusion alarm systems were born, so to speak.

Computer-controlled electronics access all of the variables in a system and allow entry only to those who know the password or code. There are many doors and windows in most houses and small businesses, so a small computer is needed to keep track of what is what, when, and where at what time.

Such security terminals now come in mini-keyboard control boxes mounted just inside the main entrance (and sometimes the rear as well). The owner is allowed a delayed entrance and exit to punch in the proper code, the time being determined by the owner. These units also use power-failure alarm circuits, act as timers and alarm clocks, and so on.

These popular systems are quite effective. Since most signal across telephone lines to security centers, they are hard to defeat. Some systems even communicate with other computer terminals throughout the premises and/or between a home and business.

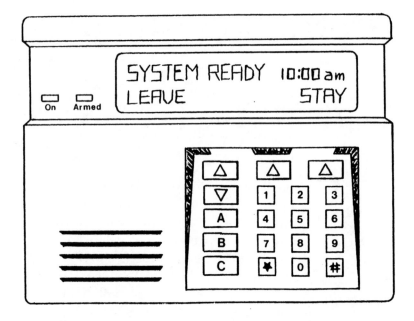

Figure 19. Security terminal.

CHAPTER 10

Photoelectric and Infrared Detectors

T he photo tube was invented near the turn of the century, but its first practical use as a detector of humans was in the late 1930s as a customer announcer in some of the larger stores of the time. In fact, one of the first true electronic intrusion alarm systems was a photo detector unit. These early systems used the visible range of the light spectrum. A light beam was focused on a vacuum tube photocell, and the light path crossed an entranceway such as a door or window. When the beam was broken by the passing of an intruder, the photocell would respond and the alarm would be tripped.

A major disadvantage of these early photo detector alarms was that the beam was visible and intruders would simply go over or under it. Dust particles or an aerosol spray were used to expose the path of the beam, making it easy to avoid. The system could also be defeated by shining an ordinary flashlight into the photocell, walking through the beam, and escaping without tripping the alarm (with booty and all). As such, many refinements to the photoelectric system were done, but it still never became very dependable with visible light.

As advances were made in the field of electronics, photoelectric systems became more integrated and it was soon discovered that infrared light (the lower end of the light spectrum that is invisible to human eyes but can be felt as warmth on the skin) maintained a narrow beam, was invisible, and could be modulated as easily as visible light. With light-emitting diodes (LEDs—see Appendix) and other solid-state electronics on the scene, infrared systems became compact, highly reliable, and sensitive. They also were reasonably priced and available to the general public by the early 1970s.

LIGHT EMITTERS

Since the LED basically has revolutionized modern electronic application, we will discuss it briefly. Light emitting diodes are solid-state lamps (the device's elements are not contained in a vacuum). The LED simply is a diode that has a high forward bias applied to it, causing a gallium arsenide chip to glow. The usual colors available are red, orange, yellow, and green (as well as infrared). Blue LEDs are not available at this time because there is a problem getting gallium arsenide molecules to vibrate that fast. Since LEDs give off little heat, they use less current— approximately 20 milliamps (.02 amperes)—and are much more efficient than regular lamps. They are also much smaller than most incandescent lamps.

LEDs were used in early hand calculators as indicator lights (liquid crystals are now widely used because they require even less current than LEDs, though they are less bright), close-range proximity sensors in industrial applications, and numerous other devices. Almost every electronic device in use today has one or more LEDs on or in it.

Infrared LEDs are used as detectors in the robotics industry. One special case is when they are used to create a safety "curtain" of infrared light in front of a shearing blade on a circuit board depaneling machine. If the operator's hands get too close to the blade, the infrared beams are broken and the blade stops.

Infrared LEDs have a built-in lens that focus the infrared light into a narrow beam. The units can be very small, some the size of the head of a pin. This makes them very difficult for intruders to locate and defeat. But the standard size for most infrared and visible-light LEDs is about an eighth of an inch in diameter.

LIGHT RECEIVERS

Infrared and visible LEDs must have counterparts— the receiver of the light—for the system to work. State-of-the-art detectors for infrared emitters are either photodiodes, photoresistors, or, more commonly, phototransistors (see Appendix). A photodiode is a light-sensitive diode that is reverse-biased and conducts when exposed to white light or infrared energy, depending on the application. A photoresistor is light-sensitive too. This device decreases its resistance with an increase of light shining on it. Instead of just switching on or off like a photodiode, a photoresistor can vary its conductivity in response to varying degrees of light.

On the other hand, a phototransistor uses its base junction as a light sensor. It usually has a built-in lens

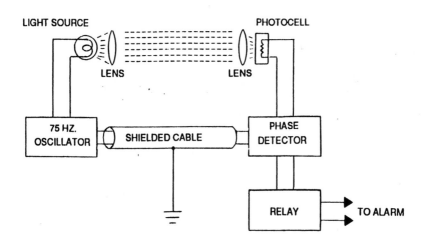

Figure 20. A modulated photoelectric alarm system.

over the top of the can or transistor package (see Appendix). When visible or infrared light hits the base, current can flow through the emitter-collector junctions, thus turning the circuit "on." The base has no electrical connection. Most systems that use broken-beam detection employ phototransistors as light receivers.

There are other photodetectors on the market, but those mentioned above are most common used. As far as intrusion alarm systems go, photoresistors are still used occasionally, but photocells (which generate a small amount of current when light strikes them) have not been used for years.

One of the main limitations of a photoelectric system is that it can be foiled by shining a flashlight into the photodetector, as was previously mentioned. The system has no way of distinguishing between the flashlight and the light beam of the system. Some infrared systems are sensitive enough in the visible portion of the light spectrum that they too can be foiled in this way.

Figure 20 is a block diagram of a photoelectric system that cannot be defeated in this way. The light source is driven by a low-frequency oscillator of about 75 Hz (or cycles per second, or cps) so the beam can be modulated at the frequency of the oscillator. The oscillator also provides a reference signal for the phase detector circuit, and the two are electronically balanced. When the reference signal from the oscillator is in phase with the signal from the photocell, the output from the phase detector will be high. The RC (resistive/capacitive network) phase shifting circuit (which actually goes between the photocell and the phase detector) compensates for any phase shifts in the system.

Now, if the light beam is interrupted, only the referenced input to the phase detector will change; the output will drop, de-energizing the relay and setting off the alarm. So the alarm can be set off by a steady beam of a flashlight if it is not modulated with (or timed and in AC phase with) the phase detector-oscillator network. The frequency of the oscillator is set low at 50 to 100 Hz. Multiples of the AC power line frequency (60 Hz) are avoided to eliminate the possibility of defeating the system by synchronizing the intruder light with the power line.

This system can be used with infrared as well. Instead of using a low-frequency oscillator, the infrared system uses a pulse generator. Also, the phase detector is replaced with a gated pulse detector. Other than that, the circuit operation is the same. In any case, these systems are difficult to foil using an external light source.

INFRARED PERIMETER PROTECTION

LEDs have the advantage of producing greater output when they are pulsed than when they're lit with a steady current. The power dissipation of an LED is very low. But by pulsing the LED's current, it is possible to achieve a

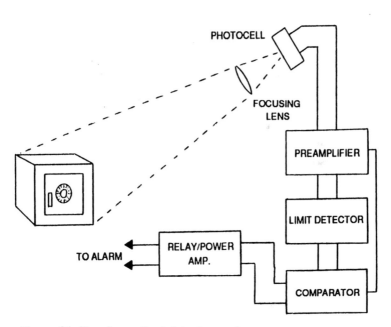

Figure 21. Passive optical detector system.

higher peak of power output (in lumens) without exceeding its average power rating.

A perimeter system using infrared beams can be set up with an LED that pulses a narrow beam of infrared energy to "watch" entrances. Mirrors can be used to direct the beam around corners and sometimes even through walls before it is picked up by the system's phototransistor. If the beam is interrupted by an intruder, the system will sound the alarm. The beam can also "crisscross" within a building, thereby making defeat of the system more difficult.

PASSIVE OPTICAL DETECTORS

Another form of the photoelectric system is the passive optical detector. This type of system does not use a light beam for its operation. Rather, it measures ambient light in the protected area and responds to any sudden changes.

The photocell is directed toward the area to be pro-

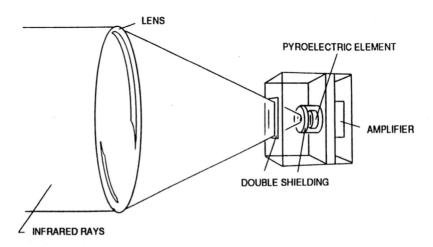

Figure 22. An exploded view of a passive infrared (PIR) sensor made as one IC chip by Optex-USA, Inc. Note built-in amplifier just behind the pyroelectric element.

tected and will not respond to any gradual changes of ambient light, such as the sun setting. Gradual changes are compensated for in the RC coupling network (signal filter) of the circuitry. But any sudden change in light, either from an addition of light or from a decrease in light caused by a burglar in the protected area, will trip the alarm. Each passive optical detector system must be fine-tuned for the particular situation. In most cases, the light from a single match will set off the alarm. Motion-detection television cameras are used in the same way.

A passive optical detector system works like this: the photocell is made up of a thin slice of silicon that, when treated, becomes sensitive to light. When an image is focused on a small bank of these silicon "cells," it sets up a series of reference voltages to the comparator circuit. A nominal voltage is amplified by the preamp. This information is in turn fed to the limit detector and when these voltages shift faster than what the comparator can respond to, a current (negative or positive) is sent through to signal the alarm. To put it in other words, the RC constant of the coupling circuit has a slow discharge rate, so any sudden changes in voltage caused by the photocells results in a voltage "override" of the RC coupling and the signal continues on to set off the alarm circuit.

INFRARED BODY HEAT DETECTORS

Another version of the passive optical detector is the infrared body heat sensor system, which, as the name implies, senses the heat of the intruder's body. Systems should be installed near corners and high on the wall (see Fig. 23). Since infrared radiation has a relatively narrow beam or pathway, several detectors usually are arranged in a flat, level spread to cover a wide area. These detectors are also adjustable to be sensitive to infrared radiation at a temperature very near 98.6°F, which is the normal temperature of the human body. Background infrared sources that lay outside the range

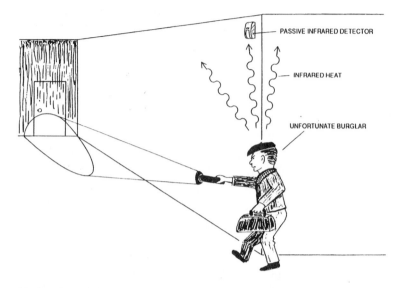

Figure 23. Passive infrared detector system should be mounted high on a wall corner for silent alarm operation.

of 98.6 degrees are filtered out of the unit's sensor.

Infrared detectors are difficult to defeat. For example, if a burglar were to use a sheet of cardboard to cover himself in order to get past the detector, the alarm would still go off because the temperature of the cardboard would be cooler than the background ambient temperature. These systems can "see" such sudden, segmented changes in temperature, particularly if a segment of the background is moving. To get the cardboard at the same temperature as the background ambient temperature would be very difficult. But this system can be foiled if one moves very slowly in the protected area.[11] Since most systems can sense only sudden changes in background ambient, this is possible.

Newer models of infrared detector systems have a wide coverage and shield out radio frequency interference. Older models could be forced into false alarm with a high-powered flashlight from outside a window, but

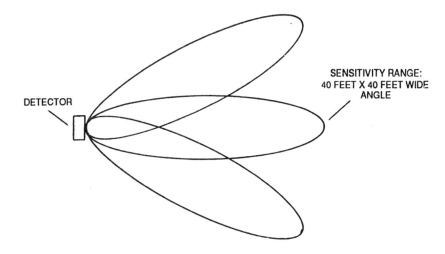

Figure 24. Sensitivity pattern of infrared body-heat detector.

today's systems employ light filters that shield out other sources of light energy. [12]

ADVANTAGES

As outlined in this chapter, each system has its own advantages, depending on the application. Choose a system that fits your budget and needs. Again, talk to a professional alarm installer.

DISADVANTAGES

One of the limitations of a photoelectric beam system is that it is difficult to apply in areas that have long, straight paths for the beam. In cases like this, a large quantity of mirrors has to be used. This often causes false alarms if the mirrors get out of alignment or become dirty. It is also possible, though difficult, for a burglar to enter an area without detection by using mirrors to deflect and reroute the beams.

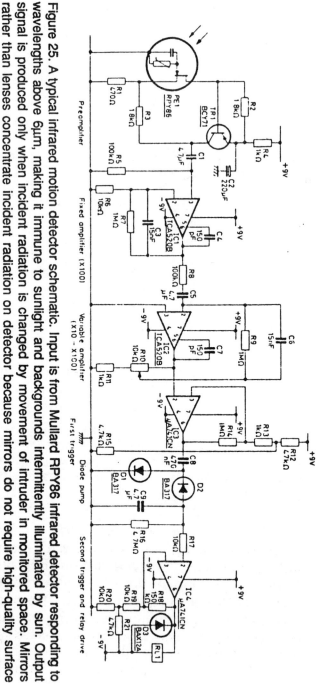

Figure 25. A typical infrared motion detector schematic. Input is from Mullard RPY86 infrared detector responding to wavelengths above 6μm, making it immune to sunlight and backgrounds intermittently illuminated by sun. Output signal is produced only when incident radiation is changed by movement of intruder in monitored space. Mirrors rather than lenses concentrate incident radiation on detector because mirrors do not require high-quality surface finish. Preamp is followed by two amplifier stages, with R10 varying gain of second stage between 10 and 100. Bandwidth is 0.3-10 Hz. First trigger, having threshold of about 1 V, drives second trigger through diode pump to energize alarm relay when intruder is present. (From *Ceramic Pyroelectric Infrared Detectors*, published by Mullard, London, 1978, Technical Note 79, TP1664, p. 8.)

68

CHAPTER 11

Ultrasonic
Intrusion Detectors

The ultrasonic Doppler alarm system has been one of the most successful intruder detectors ever made. Working on the same principle as radar, the ultrasonic system provides protection throughout an area against any moving intruder. Let's look at some basic principles of ultrasonic waves.

Ultrasonic alarm systems use audio (sound) waves in a frequency range above that of normal human hearing, usually in the range of 20 to 50 kHz (20,000-50,000 cps). As such, the system's ultrasonic transmitter produces narrow beams of sound waves that cannot be heard or felt, which makes the system difficult to detect.

It is important to realize that ultrasonic waves and radio waves are two separate forms of energy. A radio wave is an electromagnetic form of energy composed of alternating electrically induced magnetic fields. An ultrasonic wave is an acoustical pressure in a transmission medium such as air or water. Some medical applications use ultrasonic waves clear up to the 10 MHz (10 million cps) range (though this should not be mistaken for a radio wave signal in the 10 MHz range).

So if an oscillator were to produce a signal at 40 kHz (40,000 cps), for example, and feed it to an antenna, the result would be source of electromagnetic waves. But if the same 40 kHz oscillator were connected to an electromechanical transducer, then it would produce an ultrasonic wave. The difference is in the energy conversion device of the output—antenna or transducer.

Compression waves emitted from an ultrasonic transmitter are bounced off walls and furniture to be reflected back toward the ultrasonic receiver. Some of the energy is directed toward the receiver, but most of it is reflected many times off the walls and reaches the receiver at slightly different intensity and phase in relationship to the direct beams. These directed and reflected ultrasonic waves either reinforce or cancel each other out at the detector. Thus the intruder will affect the reflected waves differently in various parts of the room. This changes the phase relationship of the waves at the receiver end and sets off the alarm.

Figure 26 depicts an oversimplified view of ultrasonic energy patterns. Actually, they act like compression

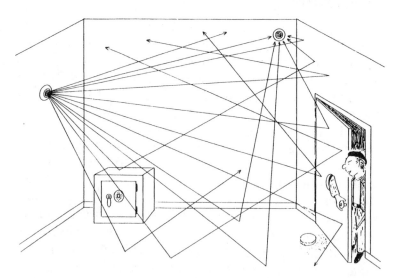

Figure 26. Ultrasonic alarm system. Standing waves are represented as arrows or direction of ultrasonic compression waves.

waves that set up a standing wave pattern like ripples in a vibrating coffee cup. When the pattern is changed by a moving object, the phase shift is detected and the alarm is sounded.

In other words, if nothing in the protected area moves, then the signal at the receiver will be constant. If an intruder comes into the protected area, the reflected signals will change in amplitude and phase relationship. This causes the signals to go into amplitude modulation at the receiver end of the ultrasonic system. This modulation is detected and the alarm is set off.

The ultrasonic intrusion alarm system should be sensitive enough to detect motion in the protected area but should not be affected by changes in air currents. The ultrasonic wave is reflected so many times from one surface to another in a protected area that motion in any direction will cause an intrusion signal and set off the alarm.

Ultrasonic systems work best in areas that have lots of hard surfaces to reflect the ultrasonic waves. Carpet, drapery, tapestries, and other wall hangings absorb sound and do not make good ultrasound reflectors. To protect rooms that have such things, other intrusion alarm systems should be considered.

TRANSDUCERS

In order to achieve an acoustical force sufficient to produce strong ultrasonic waves, a transducer is needed. A transducer converts electrical energy into mechanical energy. This mechanical vibration compresses the air into pulses corresponding to the frequency of the AC (alternating current) from the oscillator that drives it. A regular audio speaker cannot do the job because too much energy is lost as heat when certain frequencies are surpassed in wire-wound speaker coils.

There are two types of transducers used in ultrasonic alarm systems: crystal and dynamic. Crystal-type transducers use a precisely cut quartz crystal called a piezo-electric element. When AC voltage is applied across the crystal, it contracts and expands in accordance with the polarity of the current flow. This warping of the crystal produces a vibration that can be acoustic in nature (the reverse can also happen—suddenly compressing the quartz crystal will cause voltage to appear across its face).

The dynamic-type transducer operates much like a loudspeaker but is constructed more like a dynamic microphone. This transducer uses an electromagnetic coil around a movable shell about a permanent magnet. A diaphragm is attached to the coil so that when AC voltage is applied to it, the coil and diaphragm travel back and forth as the electromagnetic field oscillates, thus produc-ing an acoustical pressure wave. Although ultrasonic transducers may be similar in construction to speakers, a speaker cannot be used as one; the oscillator switches polarity too fast for the diaphragm to respond. Ultrasonic transducers are built more like microphones than speak-ers. In fact, crystal microphones are often used as such in some homemade ultrasonic burglar alarm circuits.

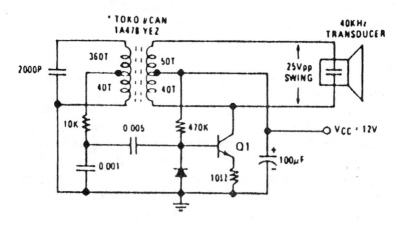

Figure 27. 40 kHz ultrasonic transmitter schematic.

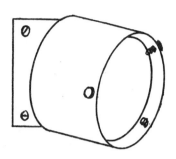

Figure 28. Ultrasonic transmitter/receiver horn.

The receiving transducer has the opposite function; it converts acoustical (sound) pressure waves into electrical signals. It also is built similarly to a microphone in a sound system but responds only to the proper frequency in the ultrasonic range. Usually identical transducers are used both as transmitter and receiver in a commercial system.

Transducers have different directional patterns. Highly directional units are used in long, narrow areas such as corridors and halls. Omnidirectional units are used to protect large, open areas.

The ultrasonic transmitter unit is composed of an oscillator (operating at the desired frequency) and a transducer. Older transmitter oscillators consist of a simple LC (inductance/capacitance network) resonator circuit. The newer or later models use an RC (resistance/capacitance network) oscillator or tuned circuit. The inductance side of the tuned circuit in Figure 27 is the left half of the transformer winding. [13] Modern transmitters also used piezoelectric tuned crystal resonators instead of coils and capacitors. The transmitter side of the ultrasonic intrusion alarm system is so simple that it is usually mounted together with the receiver in one housing. The unit is mounted on the wall near the ceiling. It is shaped much like a small tin can and has an adjustable positioning neck (see Fig. 28).

RECEIVER

The ultrasonic receiver consists of a transducer, a tuned circuit, a series of amplifiers, a detector, and an alarm trigger circuit (see Fig. 29). The transducer converts ultrasonic energy into electrical energy at the ultrasonic frequency. The input circuit is tuned to the frequency of the transmitter so that it only passes the signals close to that frequency. This narrows the bandwidth down so the system is effective in eliminating false alarms. High-frequency sounds from birds, bats, steam valves, and other miscellaneous sources cannot affect the operation of modern ultrasonic intrusion alarm systems. In other words, if the sounds are not at the sustained and precise frequency of the system, they are filtered out of the circuit.

The signal is then amplified and sent to the detector. Gain control (the amount of amplification) in the amplifier sets the sensitivity of the overall system. At this point, the signal is a minute, high-frequency audio voltage in the circuit. If nothing is moving in the protected area, the amplitude of the signal will remain consistent so that there will be no output from the detector.

When an intruder moves into the protected area, however, the ultrasonic signal is modulated by the low frequency of the shifting patterns of the reflected ultrasonic waves. This modulation is detected as a phase difference in the tuned circuit. The amplifier then passes the signal to the detector circuit, which triggers the alarm.

When the system is in proper operation, the transmitter sets up a complex network of standing waves within the protected area. These patterns of energy repeat an established path of occurrence; that is to say, phase dif-

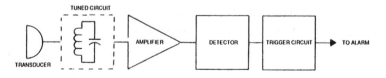

Figure 29. Basic ultrasonic receiver system.

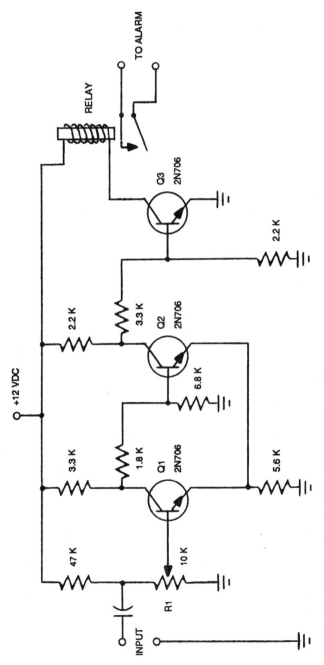

Figure 30. Schematic of a typical ultrasonic receiver.

75

ferences are set up by the repeated action of the wave patterns. These standing waves bounce back to the receiver, reflected from nearly all the objects in the protected area. When any of the waves are interrupted or redirected, the alarm will sound.

When an ultrasonic signal is modulated (either interrupted or redirected), the detector will shift its voltage output and signal the alarm. The frequency of the modulation will depend on the rate of motion of the intruder; the amplitude of the signal will depend on the total area of the intruder. After the detector there is a high-pass filter circuit that eliminates very low-frequency intrusion signals; this prevents the system from being triggered by normal air currents in the room. The adjustment of this filter creates a compromise between the condition that will detect the slowest moving intruder and one that is triggered by air current.

The filtered signal is applied to a schimdt trigger circuit (see Fig. 30). Q1 and Q2 make up the schimdt trigger. The transistor is normally off while Q2 is conducting. When an input signal exceeds a level predetermined by R1, transistor Q1 will start to conduct, shutting off Q2. This is repeated and produces a square wave output used to drive Q3. This drives the relay, turning on the alarm. The input signal has to exceed a threshold level (determined by the setting of R1) in order to produce a square wave. Below this threshold no signal can be generated.

Usually these circuits have time delays built in so that the alarm does not go off for at least ten seconds or more after the intrusion signal has been introduced. This prevents false alarms caused by radio frequency interference, curtains moving in a breeze, or even surges on the power line.

The magnitude of the intruder signal that drives Q3 depends on the area of the intruder (i.e., how big he is). But this can be adjusted to trigger the alarm even if a very small person were detected moving very slowly in the protected area. At the same time, the motion of small animals like mice or large insects will not affect the system. This setting is represented by R1 in Figure 30. [14]

HELPFUL INSTALLATION TIPS

Ultrasonic intrusion alarm systems have to be installed properly in order to offer the most protection. The positioning and location of the transmitter/receiver horn are critical for optimal performance of the system. But one of the main considerations when installing transducers is that if you are protecting an area that is rather small and rectangular in shape, remember to not point the transducer directly toward anything that moves or has moving parts, such as electric fans, forced-air heating ducts, air conditioners, or any other place where air moves.

Ultrasonic signals tend to be blocked off by large desks or other furniture and especially by partitions. This creates "blind spots" where areas are not protected. The best one can do in such a situation is to try to find the best position for the transducers, then test the area by walking slowly around within it. Also, make sure that no normal occurrence in the room will trigger the system. If you find something like this causing false alarms, then the transducers should be relocated.

Various events in our everyday lives produce ultrasonic signals. For example, bird calls have been known to unlock ultrasonic remote door locks. The rattling of a ring of keys can sometimes change the TV channel on an old-style, ultrasonic-controlled TV remote control system. Ultrasonic-controlled garage doors can sometimes be opened with an ultrasonic dog whistle. If such a situation occurs, all one has to do is adjust the tunable inductors in both the receiver and the remote-control transmitter and move the system frequency off the dog whistle's (or other source's) frequency. If, for example, you find yourself with a mysteriously opening garage door, a little deductive reasoning usually will find the source, and most door-opening systems are tunable.

Use a transducer with a proper pattern. If there are a lot of moving objects in the area, use a directional transducer. In small areas, mount the transducer near an upper corner of the room, preferably near the ceiling. It should also be mounted on a surface that is rigid and free of vibration. If the ceiling is more than twelve-feet high, the transducer should be mounted on the inside wall rather than an outside wall because of possible vibrations from outside. A transducer should also be at least ten feet from objects that emit high-pitched sounds, such as telephone bells (or beepers), radiator valves, and steam pipe valves. Also remember to keep a transducer as far as possible from other moving objects like drapes, curtains, computer fans, and machinery. Once you have mounted the transducer, set sensitivity controls for optimum performance in accordance with the manufacturer's instructions.

ADVANTAGES
Ultrasonic alarm systems have many advantages. The system is difficult to identify. It is also difficult to foil and, unlike perimeter protection systems, it will spot the "stay-behind" the instant he moves from his hiding place. Ultrasonic systems also drive out most of the rodent and insect life in the protected area because continual ultrasonic sound irritates them.

DISADVANTAGES
The main limitation of an ultrasonic system is false alarms caused by outside sources. Being that these systems operate on ultrasonic frequencies, they can be jammed or triggered by miscellaneous ultrasounds. Also, these systems cannot be used in large open areas because of the absorbing effect distance has on radiated energy. The energy needs to bounce off stable objects within its range in order for the system to operate properly. Finally, most systems can be detected by an intrud-

er if he listens with a specially designed sensitive receiver for ultrasonic frequencies. [15]

Most of the other limitations of ultrasonic systems are the result of improper installation. Essentially, each system must be engineered for each situation. In many cases, people install an ultrasonic system when they should have installed a passive infrared (PIR) detector. A $2,000 ultrasonic intrusion alarm system can be outperformed by a $500 PIR, depending on the circumstances.

CHAPTER 12

Proximity
Detectors

P roximity detectors basically are passive systems. They are activated by the naturally occurring body capacitance of the intruder. There are several types of capacitive-sensitive circuits used for this purpose.

Most other intrusion detectors are designed with precise engineering to ensure that the system will work properly when installed. The proximity detector, on the other hand, is usually a piece of wire of arbitrary length and, in some cases, can be a safe or filing cabinet (the object being protected). Of all of the different alarm systems on the market today, the proximity detector system is the most difficult to install for maximum effectiveness.

The sensing wire (or the object being protected) is the most critical part of the system because it acts as a capacitor (see Appendix), but this type of capacitance is slightly different than what is used in electronic circuits. When the intruder is in the vicinity of the proximity detector, the electrical flux that is set up between the sensor wire and the ground is interrupted. The air within the field acts as a dielectric and its dielectric constant is 1. The human body has a dielectric value of approximately 80, which is the same as water. When an intruder approaches the system, some of the electric flux will pass through his body (it cannot be sensed or felt). This has the effect of

Figure 31. Proximity detector system. The intruder becomes part of the capacitive circuit of the system, which changes the input capacitance of the proximity detector.

increasing the capacitance of the system input and setting off the alarm. Most human body fluids are electrolytes so the body is a poor dielectric.

PROXIMITY SENSING DEVICES

The actual sensing device may be a straight wire or a wire that follows a path around a building, cabinet, or other object. The actual mathematical expression of what happens is a bit complex and involves electric field theory. But there are some basic principles that can help one understand how these systems work.

It should be noted that there are four basic facts about the proper operation of capacitive proximity detectors: 1) the capacitance of the system should be stable when no intruder is present; 2) the presence of the intruder should create enough capacitive change in the system to trigger the alarm; 3) the system should not produce so much energy that it interferes with the operation of other equipment; and 4) the system should not be overly sensitive to other sources of energy such as nearby radio stations.

It should also be noted that the sensing wires should not become antennas. In fact, it is detrimental to the system if they are allowed to act as antennas. Antennas emit and receive electromagnetic energy. But capacitive proximity detectors use their sensing wire or wires as a closed electromagnetic path either to ground or to another part of the sensor circuit. If the sensor wire is longer than one-tenth of the wavelength of the frequency of operation, it will try to act like an antenna and transmit. To prevent this problem, most proximity detector systems operate at a frequency below 50 kHz. At 50 kHz, one-tenth wavelength is about 2,000 feet of sensing wire. So in this case, the above sensing wire length is the maximum one could use at that frequency.

Generally speaking, if the distance from the sensing wire to the intruder is cut in half, the change in system capacitance will be four times as great. But this is not a serious limitation because in order for the system to work properly, it doesn't have to be that sensitive. In fact, the system will work better in the long run if the sensitivity is adjusted to a few feet rather than 12 to 15 feet, which is the maximum for some high-grade systems.

Some systems designed for safes and filing cabinets are made so insensitive that the object actually has to be touched in order to trigger the alarm. Using capacitive proximity detectors as touch sensors also makes false alarms caused by mice or large insects less likely. Yet this generally is recommended only if you have other means of perimeter protection.

There are other influences that affect capacitive proximity detectors. The most common are changes in temperature and humidity of the air. In order to prevent false alarms from these variables, AC coupling is incorporated into the system itself. With this kind of filtration, the circuit will not respond to slow changes in capacitance but will respond to more rapid changes such as the sudden presence of an intruder.

Stray signals can be a problem for proximity detectors. Even though the sensing circuit is designed to be a poor antenna, it can still pick up nearby CB transmissions or radio stations. As such, low-pass filters are installed on the oscillator side of the sensing wire. Also, electric motors, walkie-talkies, and neon signs should be kept away from the proximity sensing wires.

BEAT FREQUENCY PROXIMITY DETECTORS

Since capacitive proximity detectors can be affected by temperature and humidity, beat frequency proximity detectors were designed to stop this problem. This system uses two oscillators with two separate sensing wires. The two oscillators are tuned to provide a beat frequency; that is, one oscillator is tuned to one frequency (for example, 30 kHz) while the other is tuned to a frequency that is a harmonic lower (15 kHz).

When the capacitance of one wire is changed slightly by the presence of an intruder, the difference in frequen-

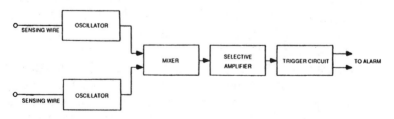

Fgure 32. Beat frequency proximity detector system.

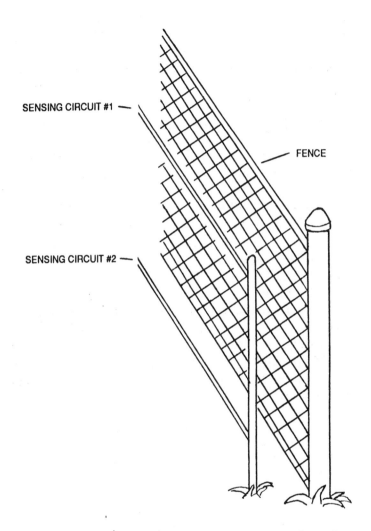

Figure 33. Beat frequency proximity detector protecting a fence.

cy between the two oscillators will cause a shift in voltage within the mixer circuit. The selective amplifier
senses this change in voltage on one side of the circuitry,
amplifies it, and sends it down to the trigger circuit,
sounding the alarm. Should equal changes occur across

both sensing leads, such as a change in temperature or humidity, there will be no resultant output of voltage from the mixer circuit and the alarm will not sound.

Beat frequency detectors are commonly used for outdoor applications. They usually are set up as two sensing wires running parallel to each other along a fence (see Fig. 33). Some systems are sensitive enough to detect an intruder up to fifteen feet away. Depending on the soil conductivity, they can even detect intruders underground who may be tunneling their way into the premises.

BRIDGE-TYPE PROXIMITY DETECTORS

One of the first proximity detector circuits ever designed used an impedance bridge (see Figure 34). With an applied AC voltage on the circuit, we have C1 over C2 equals R2 over R1:

$$C1/C2 = R2/R1$$

The overall impedance of the circuit is balanced and there is no voltage at points A and B in Figure 34. This is called the "null" condition of the circuit. Should the value of either R1 or R2 or C1 or C2 change in any way, the bridge is no longer balanced and AC voltage appears at points A and B.

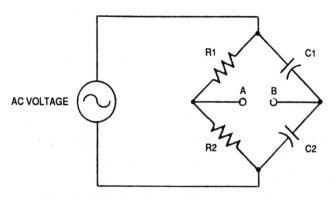

Figure 34. Basic capacitance bridge.

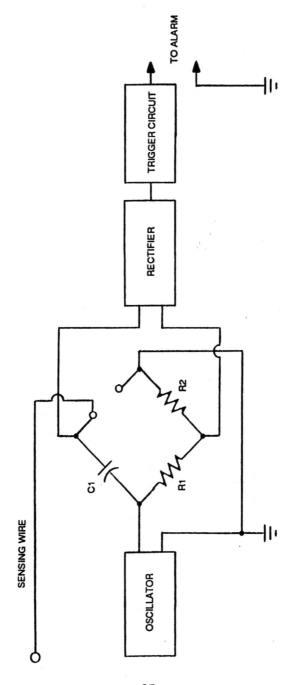

Figure 35. Bridge-type proximity detector. Note that C2 has now become the sensor wire and its relationship to ground.

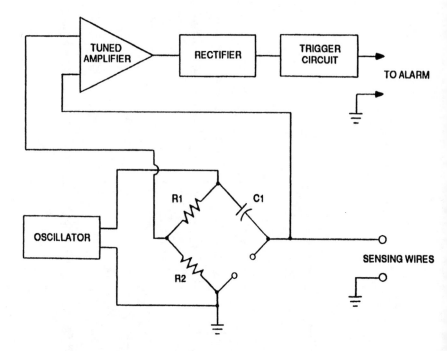

Figure 36. Improved bridge-type proximity detector.

The bridge-type proximity detector shown in Figure 35 is an example of the practical way to use the circuit in Figure 34. Note that C2 has been replaced with a sensing wire. This sensing wire acts electrically like a capacitor; that is, a charge is maintained between itself and ground. When an intruder approaches the sensing wire, the capacitance will change, throwing the bridge circuit out of balance electrically. AC voltage then appears at the output of the bridge circuit. Since the trigger circuit can only operate on a DC (or a pulsing DC) signal, the AC signal is rectified (turned into DC) by the rectifier circuit, triggering the trigger circuit and thus the alarm itself.

This circuit is a representation of one of the first proximity alarm systems used. It has several limitations, the worst being that in order to get good coverage, a very

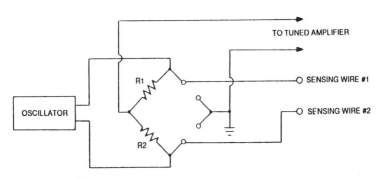

Figure 37. Bridge-type proximity detector with temperature and humidity compensation.

large signal is required from the oscillator. This, of course, will cause interference to radio and television receivers. It also makes the system very sensitive to interference, causing false alarms.

By being more selective with the use of a tuned amplifier, as illustrated in Figure 36, we can solve most of these problems. The tuned-port proximity detector is frequency selective of any incoming signals to the rectifier. It filters out all signals except those at the same frequency of the oscillator. This prevents antennalike operation of the sensor wire. It also reduces the required power of the oscillator itself, and with less power at the oscillator circuit, there is less chance of the system becoming overly sensitive and producing false alarms.

Figure 37 shows that we can improve the circuitry even more to compensate for temperature and humidity. This is done simply by replacing C1 with a second sensing wire. Temperature and humidity will affect both sides of the bridge equally, but an intruder will always affect one wire slightly more than the other—enough to throw the circuit out of null and set off the alarm.

FET PROXIMITY DETECTORS
We can simplify the process of sensing a change of

voltage across a capacitive network merely by sampling the voltage across the charged capacitive circuit. In order to do this, we need a sensing device that has a high input impedance that electronically isolates the detector from the alarm-sounding section of the circuit. An isolated gate field-effect transistor (FET for short—see Appendix) is used for such a purpose. FET proximity detectors are extremely sensitive, though, and are subject to false alarms with humidity changes. For this reason they must be installed properly, but with proper installation they are quite effective.

It must also be noted that rain can be a real problem for all types of capacitive proximity detectors. This problem can be minimized by using high-quality insulators to hold the sensing wires. The wires must also be free of small limbs and branches that may trigger a false alarm when the wind blows.

INDOOR PROTECTION

Safes, desks, and filing cabinets can be protected directly with proximity-type systems. The protected object must be made of metal though. Being metal, it becomes part of the electrical circuit and it has to be treated as a component. It is important to note that when using touch-sensitive proximity systems indoors, a good, reliable ground must be maintained, such as from a water pipe. Objects being protected must be insulated from the floor with rubber mats and must be at least six inches away from the walls. Loose cables such as lamp cords and telephone wires must be kept away to prevent false alarms. If there is a long distance from the detector circuitry to the object being protected, a coaxial cable should be used. But remember that the capacitance of the coaxial shielding will limit the number of objects you can protect with the system.

Sometimes flashtube circuits (the kind used in photography) are set up and driven by a low-frequency pulse

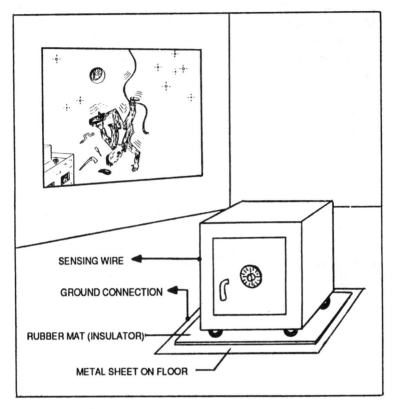

Figure 38. Protecting metal objects with proximity detectors.

generator, with the input signal being controlled by the body capacitance of the intruder. When the intruder touches something like a safe or file cabinet, his body capacitance will offset the circuit capacitance and trigger a brilliant flash into his eyes—maybe even take his photograph. Being photographed on the job is not exactly a burglar's best career move.

ADVANTAGES

Proximity intrusion detectors are great for protecting individual objects. Another good feature of these systems is that the protective case itself can be made part of the protected circuit so that any attempt to defeat the system will initiate an alarm. Proximity detectors are also quite versatile and can be used to protect just about anything with metal. Jewelry stores sometimes use them to protect jewelry cases even during business hours; they are set to sound a bell or buzzer within the store to alert the clerks that someone is browsing near them.

DISADVANTAGES

Proximity intrusion detectors are supersensitive and thus are subject to false alarms, more so than with most other systems. Also, they are inconvenient to install. You can't just plug one in, set it on the shelf, and walk away. Basically the system has to be engineered for each particular situation. This should always be done by qualified personnel.

CHAPTER 13

Microwave
Intrusion Alarms

icrowave intrusion detectors work on the same principle as Doppler radar. Their operation is also similar to that of ultrasonic intrusion detector systems, except that ultrasonic systems use sound pressure waves in the air. Microwave systems use very short radio waves. Sometimes these systems are referred to as radar alarms because that is essentially how they operate.

Microwave intrusion detectors work on the same principle as the effect a passing airplane has on a television receiver. The TV transmitter's broadcast signals are a combination of direct waves and indirect or reflected waves. Everything is okay when the TV antenna is receiving signals from both direct and reflected waves. But when an airplane flies overhead, some of the transmitted signals are reflected off it at the same rate that it is traveling. This causes amplitude modulation at the TV receiver, making the picture flutter or shift.

Similar to an ultrasonic intrusion alarm system, two separate signals arrive at the microwave alarm's receiver simultaneously. One of the signals is direct from the transmitter, caused by the direct radiation of the transmitter itself or sometimes by a direct mechanical connection. The other source of the signal is a combination of many reflected signals from the various surfaces of the

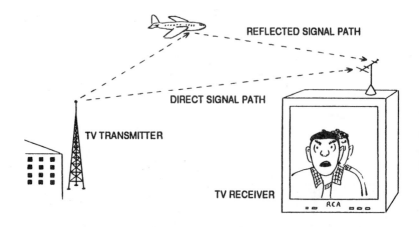

Figure 39. Microwave intruder detection systems work on the same principle as the shifting of the TV signal (double image, or "ghost," on the screen) caused by the overhead passing of an airplane.

protected area. As long as nothing moves in the protected area, the signal phase relationship is constant at the receiver. When an intruder enters the area, the shifting pattern of reflected waves results in a phase shift at the receiver end (and the modulated rate depends on the speed of the intruder).

Though the principles of microwave and ultrasonic systems seem identical, the difference lies in the medium each uses to transmit and receive energy. As was mentioned before, in ultrasonic systems the signals are air pressure waves. Generally, these waves are reflected by hard surfaces and absorbed by soft surfaces. On the other hand, microwaves are high-frequency electromagnetic waves that vibrate faster than radio waves. They are reflected well by metal surfaces but pass through most interior building materials such as wallboard, glass, and wood. In a way this is an advantage in that several rooms or offices can be protected with one system—something that cannot be done with ultrasonic alarm systems. The disadvantage to this effect is that it makes microwaves difficult to contain. Since they pass through glass quite easily, a moving automobile outside the building can cause a false alarm.

It should also be noted here that microwaves are radio waves and are not affected by air currents produced by heaters, fans, or radiator steam valves.

Microwave systems use directional antennas to help eliminate false alarms caused by moving objects outside of the intended protected area. Since it is easier to contain a higher-frequency signal than a low-frequency one, directional horns of 20,000 MHz (20,000,000,000 cps) or more are used. The wavelength of that is about .625 inches, which helps keep the transmitter horn to a workable size. (It should be noted that the term "horn" in this case is the directional transmit/receive channel of the microwave system. These horns are similar in design to those used on aircraft and ship radar systems.)

Some microwave intrusion alarm systems use parabolic reflector-type antennas. But these antennas have a tendency to spread their beam out too much, making it hard to contain the system. In most cases horns are used, and they have the dual function of being both transmitter and receiver all in one unit. This system is designed to be directional for more precise protection.

Dual-purpose horns are quite convenient. Direct signals from the transmitter bounce back to the same horn, which stops transmitting just long enough to receive the returned signal. Upon receiving the information that bounced back, the transmitter transmits again—again to shut down to receive the returned signal. This happens repeatedly in microseconds. This is called a single antenna system and, like modern aircraft radar, allows one antenna to have a dual purpose.

BISTATIC MICROWAVE SYSTEMS

A bistatic microwave system uses a separate transmitter and receiver located at two different places within the protected area. For example, the transmitter might be located at one corner of the room while the receiving antenna might be located at the other corner of the same wall. This system not only works on the same principle of Doppler radar, it can also be set off by the interruption of the microwave beam between the transmitter and receiver. The major advantage of this type of system is that there is a greater range of protection of the area.

MICROWAVE ANTENNAS

Microwave intrusion alarm systems use either horn-type antennas or parabolic reflector types similar to the ones used in microwave communications. The horn antennas are the most widely used because the beam can be more self-contained and is less likely to cause false alarms by overextending the protected area. This usually

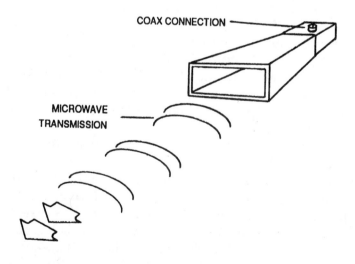

COAX CONNECTION

MICROWAVE
TRANSMISSION

Figure 40. Rectangular horn antenna.

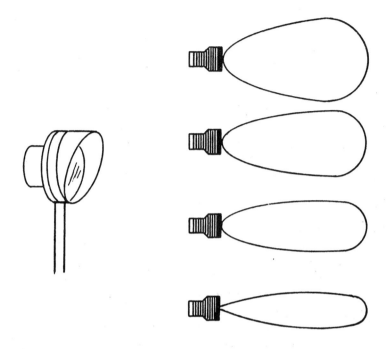

Figure 41. A 10-gigahertz (GHz) microwave antenna with typical directional patterns.

occurs along the lobes of the protective beam rather than at the end of it.

TYPICAL MICROWAVE CIRCUIT

Microwave alarm systems use very low levels of RF (radio frequency) energy. As such, solid-state electronics allow the use of a variety of circuits available to the home/business owner. An example of the most popular type is illustrated in schematic form in Figure 42. [16] This system is a microwave Doppler intrusion alarm and uses a Mullard CL8960 X-band radar module. It can detect movement of a remote target by monitoring Doppler shift in microwave radiation reflected from the target. The

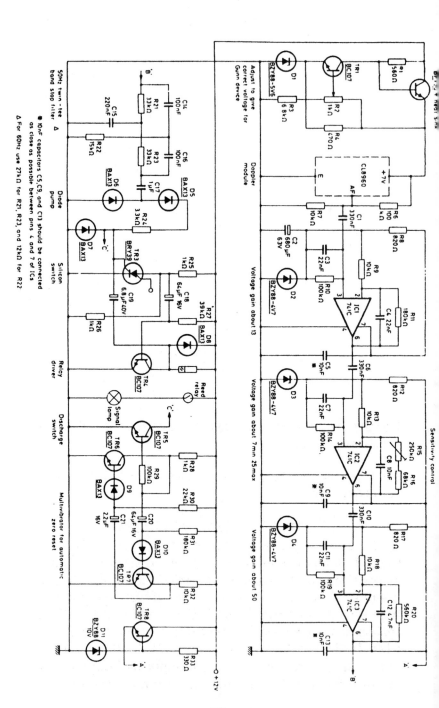

98

module consists of a Gunn diode (a type of tunnel diode used in high-frequency electronics) oscillator cavity that produces the energy needed to drive the transmitter horn. The module is mounted alongside the mixer cavity and combines the reflected energy with a sample of the oscillator signal. This sets up a time base, or reference, for the system.

The transmitted frequency is 10.7 GHz (10,700,000,000,000 cps or Hz). The Doppler change is about 31 Hz for a relative velocity of .45 meters per second (or about 1 MPH—a slow walk) between object and module. This translates as an audio frequency (AF) modulation, and this system can sense objects moving up to 400 MPH. Filtered AF is applied through the diode pump to trigger the SCR labeled TR3. This makes the contacts of the reed relay switch open for about one second. This relay action is repeated as long as the intruder is in the protected area.

HELPFUL INSTALLATION TIPS

Microwave intrusion alarm systems are effective protection if properly set up and installed (sound familiar?).

Figure 42 (left). Typical microwave intrusion alarm schematic. Mullard CL8960 X-band Doppler radar module detects movement of remote target by monitoring Doppler shift in microwave radiation reflected from target. Module consists of Gunn oscillator cavity producing energy to be radiated, mounted alongside mixer cavity that combines reflected energy with sample of oscillator signal. Transmitted frequency is 10.7 GHz. Doppler change is about 31 Hz for relative velocity of 0.45 m/s (1 MPH) of relative velocity between object and module, giving AF output for velocities up to 400 MPH. Filtered AF is applied through diode pump to trigger of silicon-controlled switch TR3 that makes contacts of reed relay open for about 1 s. Relay action is repeated as long as intruder is in monitored area. (From *Microwave Doppler Intruder Alarms*, by J.E. Saw, published by Mullard, London, 1976, Technical Information 36, TP1570, p. 6.)

Poor installation allows for easy defeat of the system. With microwave systems, they either work 100 percent or don't work at all. With improper installation there is also a tendency for false alarms.

It is important to know that a microwave antenna should be mounted at least eight feet above the floor. This allows for good coverage and also keeps it out of the way of being bumped or knocked out of alignment. Once the antenna has been set up, you don't want to move it. The surface that it is mounted on should be free of vibration.

Microwave energy passes easily through most walls to protect more than one room. The signals can pass through two plasterboard walls and even more insulated plywood walls, depending on the system. Brick, concrete, and masonry block out most of the radiated energy. Care must be taken to avoid pointing the antenna at wooden exterior walls, wooden doors, and glass windows because objects or people passing outside will cause false alarms.

Moving metallic objects like fan blades and venetian blinds (prone to movement by the wind) can also cause false alarms. If a fan must be used in the area and it has metal blades, a wire screen can be placed in front of it (some fans have this feature built around the blades or you could use one with plastic blades), preventing the microwave system from "seeing" the moving fan blades. Make certain that the screen does not vibrate or this too will set off the alarm.

It is also important to note that microwave systems can be fine-tuned by repositioning the antenna so that selective coverage of different parts of the protected perimeter can be maintained. In other words, the system can be set up to "see," say, an intruder entering a metal door on one side of a wall. Though this creates "dead zones," an intruder may enter the building from the other side and end up walking right into the microwave beam, setting off the alarm. The antenna can only see in a narrow path so sometimes multiple antenna setups are required in order to eliminate such blind spots.

Remember that metal objects are opaque to microwaves, so metal desks, filing cabinets, and room dividers should not be lined up so as to create a blind for burglars to utilize. All such objects have to be lined up along a wall with very little gap in between to prevent blind spots.

One should thoroughly test the system upon installation to prevent any false alarms. This may include having friends or family walk past outside doors as well as perform other suspicious activity to confirm proper installation.

ADVANTAGES

A microwave intrusion alarm system is an expression of state-of-the-art electronic protection. If properly installed, it is extremely difficult to foil. It also has the advantage of being able to protect more than one room with a single system. The "stay-behind" burglar will invariably wander into the system if it is properly planned out and installed. Microwave systems are also safe to the human body if the power is kept low (10 mw/cm2 or lower). [17]

DISADVANTAGES

One of the major disadvantages is that microwave systems are difficult to install properly, requiring highly trained technicians. Another disadvantage is that the signals are hard to contain within the protected area. Most office buildings have many large windows, and birds have been known to set off microwave systems just by flying past a window.

Microwave systems can also be affected by air traffic control radar. If there is a radar-producing source in the building, be certain that your microwave system is on a different frequency.

Any device that emits RF energy such as a microwave intrusion alarm system can both cause interference and be affected by interference. The Federal Communications Commission (FCC) carefully regulates such devices. The FCC has ruled that microwave intrusion alarm systems are "field disturbance sensors" since they operate on the principle of the disturbance of electromagnetic fields. [18] More information about this can be found in the publication *FCC Rules and Regulations*, part 15, available from the U.S. Government Printing Office, Washington, DC, 20402.

If for any reason you decide to build your own microwave alarm system from scratch (not recommended unless you are familiar with radio circuit design), it must be certified and labeled in accordance with FCC rules.

CHAPTER 14

Automotive Alarm Systems

uto theft is the most common type of burglary in this country. Automobiles are especially vulnerable because the auto itself is a means of escape for the thief. Yet for a reasonable cost, most car thefts can be prevented. The market is loaded with affordable electronic protection devices.

Most car thefts are done by professionals. Even though he is in a different class than a professional burglar, the professional car thief can do his job even quicker. Amateur car thieves are usually caught; the joy ride usually ends with abandonment of the car and its return to the proper owner. But professional auto thieves will steal the car and turn it over to an underground garage, where it will be stripped down for parts within the hour—forever lost to the owner. A professional auto thief can hot-wire a car in under a minute, so it is best to do as much as possible to increase the time it would take to steal the car. If the professional cannot drive away in less than two minutes, he will move on to easier pickings.

Fortunately, police departments across the country are linked up to a nationwide computer network and whenever a vehicle is stolen, that information is entered into it. Then it is just a matter of time before the car is located. For this reason, the professional auto thief has to steal the car and get rid of it as soon as possible. If the vehicle appears to be difficult to steal or if its security system is foreign to the thief, he will move on. Another major deterrent to auto theft is the attention-getting alarm. No thief wants to attract attention.

IGNITION PROTECTION

Most older cars can be hot-wired quite readily, even by some amateur auto thieves. But older vehicles can be protected by the "hot fuse circuit" method.[19] Here is how it works.

A fuse is installed and hidden between the ignition switch and the hot side of the ignition coil. From the ignition coil side of the fuse, an insulated wire is run to a hidden switch anywhere on the car. The other side of this

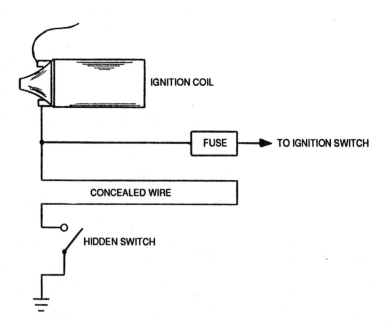

IGNITION COIL

FUSE → TO IGNITION SWITCH

CONCEALED WIRE

HIDDEN SWITCH

Figure 43. Auto ignition protection system.

switch goes to ground (the auto body). When the car is parked in a high-crime area, all the owner has to remember is to throw the hidden switch when he locks the doors. Should a thief pick the lock of or jump the ignition switch, the current path will go from the battery through the ignition switch through the fuse and then through the concealed switch to ground. This shorts out the system and blows the fuse. Most thieves will abandon the idea of stealing that car because it won't start. But even if the professional decides to jumper directly from the battery to the ignition coil, the wire he is using will heat up to melting point since he is shorting the battery to ground. This is usually enough to discourage any thief. This is a very effective and inexpensive way to prevent your car from being stolen, especially if you own an older model. Make certain you use heavy-gauge insulated wire for the "concealed wire" in Figure 43. It should be about 7 to 8 gauge to ensure that it doesn't melt when the battery is shorted to the coil.

New cars are very difficult to hot-wire. Nearly all of them use sophisticated electronic ignition systems, and though they are not foolproof, they are certainly fool-resistant. An amateur attempting to steal such a vehicle without knowledge of the newer circuitry would be a fool anyway.

Newer cars also have recessed ignition cylinders to make picking them burdensome. This also helps to prevent the cylinder from being extracted and the wires shorted out in the back of it to start the car. Ignition wiring is also armored with metal-flex cable sheathing, which makes hot-wiring more difficult.

ELECTRONIC COMBINATION AUTO LOCKS

Some newer automakers are installing electronic combination locks in the car doors and dashboard.[20] These are electrically installed in series with the auto ignition itself. Many of them require a four- or five-digit

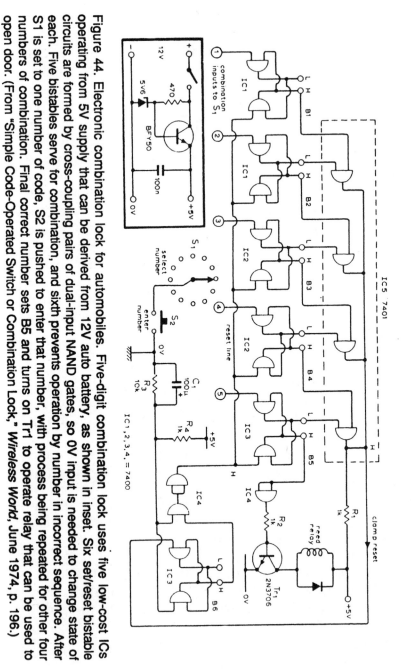

Figure 44. Electronic combination lock for automobiles. Five-digit combination lock uses five low-cost ICs operating from 5V supply that can be derived from 12V auto battery, as shown in inset. Six set/reset bistable circuits are formed by cross-coupling pairs of dual-input NAND gates, so 0V input is needed to change state of each. Five bistables serve for combination, and sixth prevents operation by number in incorrect sequence. After S1 is set to one number of code, S2 is pushed to enter that number, with process being repeated for other four numbers of combination. Final correct number sets B5 and turns on Tr1 to operate relay that can be used to open door. (From "Simple Code-Operated Switch or Combination Lock," Wireless World, June 1974, p. 196.)

106

code to start the vehicle. Some use LED readouts for the owner's convenience. These systems usually have a back-up feature that shuts the lock down for ten to twenty minutes if a code has been entered more than three times in a row. Circumventing such a deterrent would require direct knowledge of the electronic systems of that particular car. The chances that a thief has that information for that particular car are highly remote. The output switching is armored as well to prevent tampering.

TRUNK AND HOOD LOCKS

Most professional car thieves know that if they can get the hood of the car open and disconnect the battery, the auto alarm will be shut off. This can be done in seconds on most cars. With the alarm off, the thief can quickly find the alarm system wiring, cut it, and jump the ignition. But this takes more time with a dependable hood chain lock (even though the chain can be cut)— more time then most car thieves want to spend.

Some alarm systems have a backup battery in the trunk of the car. This greatly reduces the risk of the car being stolen in this manner. But some trunk locks can easily be punched out and opened with a large screwdriver. If this is a concern for you, check with your local locksmith about improving your trunk lock mechanism. Lock cylinders with heavy mounting flanges on the face of the lock and armored body construction cannot be opened easily.

ACCESSORY PROTECTION

New cars are expensive, and it's unfortunate that we have to go to all this trouble to protect them from theft. Tires, stereos, and CBs are stolen just as readily as the autos themselves. Special nuts and bolts can be used to protect these items effectively simply because they require special tools. See your local auto parts dealer or hardware store. Special lug nuts are available, for instance, to make stealing tires a specialized endeavor.

SHAKER SWITCHES

One of the most effective ways of protecting the accessories of the car and the car itself is with "shaker switches."[21] Should the car be bumped or jolted in any way, such as by opening or closing a door or jacking it up to remove tires, the sensitive switch will close and sound the alarm. Since shaker switches are small enough to be concealed easily within the car, their detection and defeat by a thief is very unlikely.

Mercury switches are also used to help prevent a vehicle from being jacked up to be towed, having a "midnight tire rotation," having the transmission stolen, and so on. The main disadvantage of a mercury switch is that one cannot use it when parked on a hill.

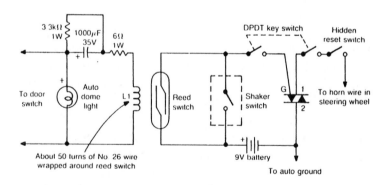

Figure 45. Shaker switch alarm system. The dome light current through L1 closes reed switch and sounds alarm. Shaker switch also activates alarm.

OVERALL AUTO THEFT PROTECTION

Although no single protection device is 100-percent effective against auto theft, the previously mentioned devices can certainly decrease your chances of being a

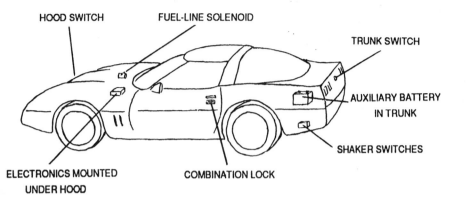

HOOD SWITCH FUEL-LINE SOLENOID

TRUNK SWITCH

AUXILIARY BATTERY
IN TRUNK

SHAKER SWITCHES

ELECTRONICS MOUNTED
UNDER HOOD

COMBINATION LOCK

Figure 46. Complete automobile protection system.

victim. Yet another device in the war against auto theft is
the in-line solenoid fuel valve. These are electrically controlled valves installed in the fuel line and operated by a
hidden switch. If the car is stolen, the thief won't get far
because the car will soon appear to have run out of gas.

Figure 46 shows the various systems that can be used
to protect the automobile. This car is so well-protected
that if someone spits on it an alarm will sound. To prevent the battery from running down, there is a time delay
to shut the alarm off shortly after tampering has stopped.
Also, there is an emergency battery in the securely locked
trunk; should the thief disconnect the battery under the
hood the alarm will still sound (never hurts to have a little extra battery power anyway). And even if the car is
stolen, it will "run out of gas" shortly after it is started
because of the fuel-line solenoid.

Some automobile cellular telephone systems are
designed to emit a coded radio transmission should the
auto be tampered with or stolen. These transmissions can
be monitored by one's security company.

Newer protection systems (including locks) utilize
remote control to turn them on or off from a short distance. The owner can also arm the device from a short

distance should he see someone attempting to steal the vehicle. These systems also make convenient panic alarms should the owner be attacked near the car.

CHAPTER 15

Power-Failure Alarms

security system without a power-failure alarm or backup is a security system that the intruder can shut off. Should the power fail by other means or should a burglar disconnect the power to the premises, the alarm system is useless. For this reason many electronic security alarm systems use a backup power source, namely self-contained power batteries.

BATTERIES

Backup batteries not only keep the alarm system on when the power fails, they also charge the power-failure alarm itself. Most systems operate with rechargeable batteries—whenever normal AC power is on, a small amount of current trickles into the cells, thereby maintaining a full charge at all times. Should the power shut down, a relay (in most cases) opens up and latches on with closed contacts in series with the battery and output signaling circuit. A reset switch then needs to be operated to release the relay and put the circuit back into normal operation. [22]

Systems that use sealed lead acid "gel-cells" as their rechargeable power source need not be concerned with battery maintenance until after four years. After that, the batteries should be checked yearly and replaced after six or seven years.

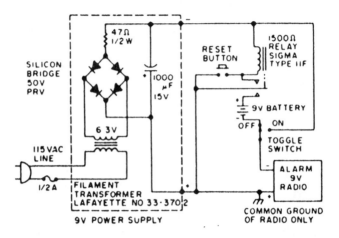

Figure 47. Power failure detector system schematic. If the power fails, the radio alarm goes on—no loud siren, bell, or whistle. Even if the power is restored, the alarm stays on until the reset button is pushed.

For best battery operation, the full charge for lead acid gel-cells (6 volts) should be from 7 to 7.5 volts. A 12-volt system should be charged with 13.5 to 14 volts. Sealed lead acid gel-cells should be replaced if they cannot hold a full charge of 6 and 12 volts respectively. Some newer gel-cells last up to eight years on standby.

Lithium battery backup systems do not get recharged but have a ten-year shelf life. If they must be used for four hours, however, chances are they will have lost about one-third of their shelf life.

Battery technology is advancing rapidly, and by the time you read this, even better batteries are probably on the market. But for all practical purposes, lead acid gel-cells are the most cost-effective and dependable power source.

Some power-failure alarm systems can keep track of how long the power was out. This information may be important for prosecution. Figure 47 is a schematic of

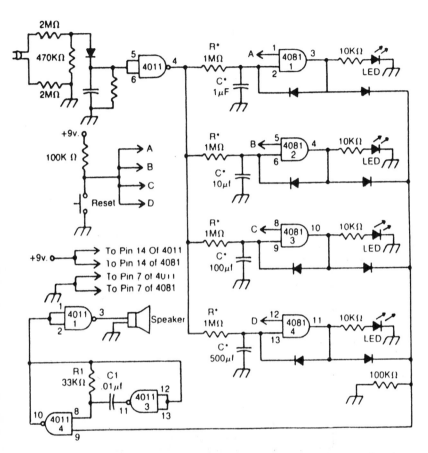

Figure 48. A more sophisticated power failure detector circuit. The circuit indicates that a power outage occurred for 1, 10, 100, or 500 seconds with the values given for R* and C*. After a power failure, the circuit can be reset by pushing the reset button.

such a system. This unit lets the home/business owner know approximately how long the power was off, whether it was for 1, 10, 100, or 500 seconds, depending on which LED is lit. The components indicated as R and C are the RC constant (resistance x capacitance)—time = R:C—needed to determine the time of response for each

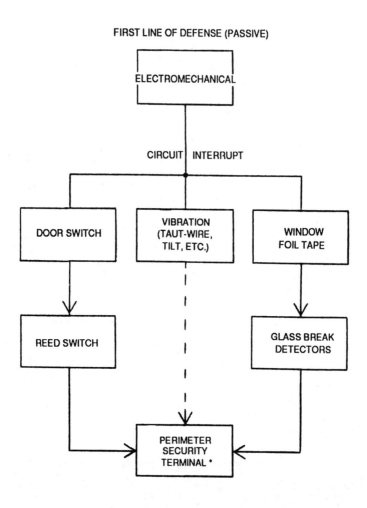

FIRST LINE OF DEFENSE (PASSIVE)

ELECTROMECHANICAL

CIRCUIT INTERRUPT

DOOR SWITCH

VIBRATION
(TAUT-WIRE,
TILT, ETC.)

WINDOW
FOIL TAPE

REED SWITCH

GLASS BREAK
DETECTORS

PERIMETER
SECURITY
TERMINAL *

* THE RESULT OF TWO OR MORE SYSTEM
TECHNOLOGIES MERGING.

Figure 49. Family of most widely used alarm systems (above and right).

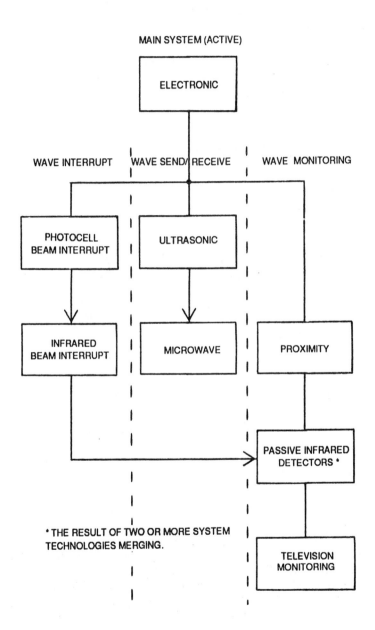

section of the circuit. After the power has been off, the circuit can be reset by the "reset" button.[23]

So all high-security alarm systems should be protected by a backup power-failure alarm. This "back door" to your system must be kept locked in order to prevent defeat by the professional burglar.

Remember, it is illegal to use deadly traps designed to kill or maim an intruder. But in Figure 50, Billy the Burglar doesn't get away this time.

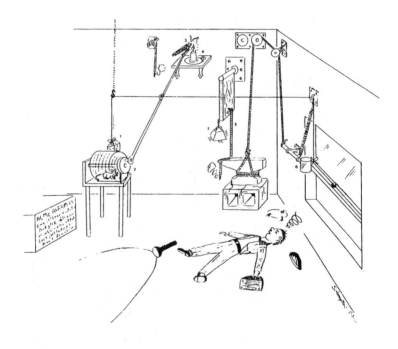

Figure 50. Cheese detector alarm system. 1) Burglar opens window, which lowers cheese to mouse's cage. 2) Mouse turns cage with cam that runs rod back and forth, which 3) strikes a match against the file, which lights the candle that 4) burns the rope holding up the anvil. 5) The anvil falls, powering the mallet that 6) coldcocks the intruder, flipping him into the room and 7) ringing the cow bell.

Conclusion

I must stress the importance of having qualified alarm installation personnel evaluate your particular situation. This book alone will not help you to completely protect your premises against intruders, but it will give you some basic guidelines.

If you bought this book in order to learn how to defeat intrusion alarm systems, then you will find that it is not complete in that way either. I only mention how to defeat outdated systems, which gives us a clear idea of the evolution of these systems. It is also fun to muse about how one might defeat some current systems.

Most importantly, remember to test your system and check for signs of wear or deterioration regularly.

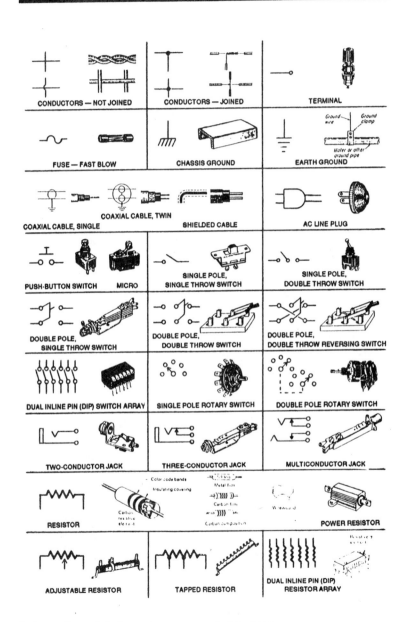

Schematic symbols and component drawings.

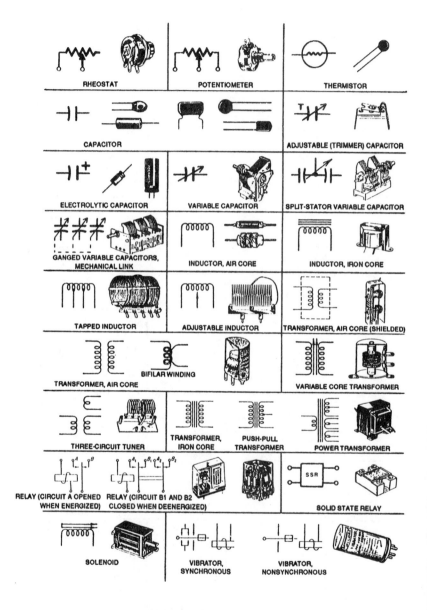

Schematic symbols and component drawings.

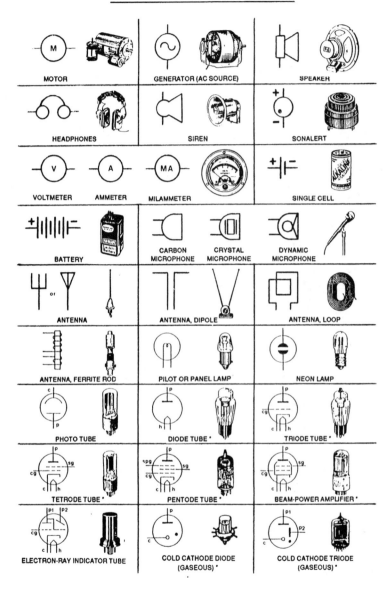

MOTOR	GENERATOR (AC SOURCE)	SPEAKER
HEADPHONES	SIREN	SONALERT
VOLTMETER AMMETER MILAMMETER		SINGLE CELL
BATTERY	CARBON MICROPHONE CRYSTAL MICROPHONE DYNAMIC MICROPHONE	
ANTENNA	ANTENNA, DIPOLE	ANTENNA, LOOP
ANTENNA, FERRITE ROD	PILOT OR PANEL LAMP	NEON LAMP
PHOTO TUBE	DIODE TUBE *	TRIODE TUBE *
TETRODE TUBE *	PENTODE TUBE *	BEAM-POWER AMPLIFIER *
ELECTRON-RAY INDICATOR TUBE	COLD CATHODE DIODE (GASEOUS) *	COLD CATHODE TRIODE (GASEOUS) *

c = cathode
h = heater (filament)
p = plate

sg = screen grid
cg = control grid
spg = suppression grid

* Tube housing styles are interchangeable.

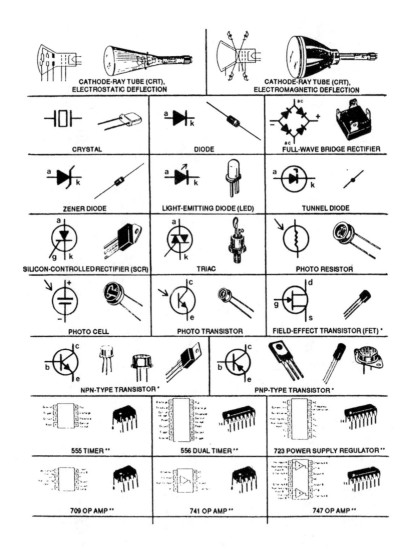

CATHODE-RAY TUBE (CRT), ELECTROSTATIC DEFLECTION

CATHODE-RAY TUBE (CRT), ELECTROMAGNETIC DEFLECTION

CRYSTAL

DIODE

FULL-WAVE BRIDGE RECTIFIER

ZENER DIODE

LIGHT-EMITTING DIODE (LED)

TUNNEL DIODE

SILICON-CONTROLLED RECTIFIER (SCR)

TRIAC

PHOTO RESISTOR

PHOTO CELL

PHOTO TRANSISTOR

FIELD-EFFECT TRANSISTOR (FET) *

NPN-TYPE TRANSISTOR *

PNP-TYPE TRANSISTOR *

555 TIMER **

556 DUAL TIMER **

723 POWER SUPPLY REGULATOR **

709 OP AMP **

741 OP AMP **

747 OP AMP **

a = anode
b = base
c = collector
g = gate

d = drain
e = emitter
k = cathode

* Transistor case styles are interchangeable.
** Integrated circuit (IC)

1. John Cunningham, *Understanding Security Electronics*: Indianapolis, IN, Howard W. Sams, 1989.

2. Ibid.

3. Ibid.

4. Ibid.

5. Mike Kessler, *Tricks of the Burglar Alarm Trade*: Boulder, CO, Paladin Press, 1990.

6. Cunningham, *Security Electronics*.

7. John Markus, *Modern Electronic Circuits Reference Manual:* New York, NY, Kingsport Press, 1980.

8. Conversation with John Angelos, 1982.

9. Rudolf Graf, *The Encyclopedia of Electronic Circuits*: Blue Ridge Summit, PA, Tab Books, Inc., 1985.

10. Markus, *Circuits Reference*.

11. Cunningham, *Security Electronics*.

12. Markus, *Circuits Reference*.

13. Graf, *Electronic Circuits*.

14. Cunningham, *Security Electronics*.

15. Charles Rakes, "Build the Ultrasonic Receiver," *Popular Electronics*, February 1989, page 46-48.

16. Markus, *Modern Electronic*.

17. Cunningham, *Security Electronics*.

18. Ibid.

19. Ibid.

20. Markus, *Electronic Circuits*.

21. Graf, *Electronic Circuits*.

22. Ibid.

23. Markus, *Electronic Circuits*.